Work at Sea, See the World:

An Insider's Secrets to the Working Life on a Cruise Ship

NANCY SOULÉ

Copyright © 2023 Nancy Soulé
All rights reserved
First Edition

NEWMAN SPRINGS PUBLISHING
320 Broad Street
Red Bank, NJ 07701

First originally published by Newman Springs Publishing 2023

ISBN 978-1-68498-178-6 (Paperback)
ISBN 978-1-68498-179-3 (Digital)

Printed in the United States of America

To my courageous mother, who relished a sailing challenge, my seafaring father who passed her legacy on to me, and to my sister who shares our passion for the wind and the sea.

Please help to protect our life-sustaining oceans. Please support http://oceanconservancy.org, and I encourage you to contribute. This nonprofit organization is creating science-based solutions to support a healthy ocean and its wildlife. By providing international programs, they are dedicated to sustainability and climatic balance. Please help us protect our magnificent oceans and the vast array of wildlife, which are depending on you. Thank you.

In addition, please visit http://4ocean.com/pages/about to see a video about how 4Ocean is dedicated to eliminating the blight of plastics and trash. Every purchase from this organization guarantees the removal of a pound of debris and provides funds for education that encourages the reduction of our dependance on plastics.

For information on the author's other publications, please visit http://www.nancysoule.net. Details on her vocal services may be found at http://soulesounds.webs.com.

CONTENTS

Introduction: Watch the Telltales ix
Chapter 1: This Is Not Just a Regular Job! 1
Chapter 2: Give It a Try 8
Chapter 3: How to Get the Job 16
Chapter 4: What You Need to Know About Living Onboard 30
Chapter 5: So You Got the Job! Now What? 33
Chapter 6: What Do You Do About Leaving Home? 36
Chapter 7: Packing and Traveling 47
Chapter 8: How Do You Sign On? 67
Chapter 9: Welcome Aboard! 80
Chapter 10: What's All This About Trainings and Drills? 87
Chapter 11: What Really Happens Below Decks? 101
Chapter 12: Any Special Advice for New Hires? 114
Chapter 13: What Crazy Things PAX Do! 121
Chapter 14: What About the Weather? 134
Chapter 15: Is There a Doctor in the House? 141
Chapter 16: Can You Get Off in the Ports? 146
Chapter 17: Life Flows on Within You and Without You 157
Chapter 18: What is Dry Dock? 160
Chapter 19: How Do You Get Outa Here? 169
Chapter 20: So What Happens When It's Over? 174
Chapter 21: Will This Job Help You as a Landlubber? 176
Chapter 22: What Happened to Ships in 2020? 187
Chapter 23: So What to Do Next? 209
Chapter 24: A Few Afterwords for the Over Forties 222
Acknowledgments 225
Appendix 227

INTRODUCTION

Watch the Telltales

As a squall whipped the waves into undulating mountains, my father braced one foot on the seat of the cockpit with his hands gripping the giant wooden wheel, healing the 40-foot sailboat as far into the wind as he could get it. Dipping the rails dangerously close to the water, the teak decks of the Flying Dutchman were slick with spray as the shiny black hull sliced through the surging waves. His face glowing with delight, he hauled the main sheet even tighter on the winch, tipping the mast farther over. I clung to the staysail for dear life, knowing he was in "the zone" and I would have to just hold on! The look on his face has stayed with me ever since as evidence of one of the happiest days of his life. He really, really wanted to buy that boat, but a graduation from tiller to wheel on bigger vessels just wasn't in his future.

> *Being outside with the wind in his face brushed away the memories nibbling continuously at the corners of his mind.* (Daniel James Brown, *The Boys in the Boat*)

I have always loved boats. Sailboats. I grew up among them: big ones, little ones, even rowboats with sails. The fickle directions of the wind have been driving me ever since. The key to successful sailing is reading the telltales, the small bits of yarn or cloth tied to the staysails, that show the wind direction. Charting a proper course can make all the difference in where you end up. In the 1930s, before I was even an idea, my mother had been a devoted competitive sailor. As the first female member admitted to the Seattle Yacht Club, she took to the waves among the boys who ferociously sailed Star-class boats on Lake Washington. Enduring the teasing, she proved herself to be an accomplished skipper, a good-natured loser, and eventually, a consistent winner. She even braved the unpredictable waters and erratic weather of the three-day Vancouver Pacific International Yacht Association regatta of 1938. And she showed those boys—she took home the trophy!

After she married my father, he was hired to move inland for an architectural job to design and build the "Hotpoint House of the Future" in Pasco, Washington. She flatly refused to become a landlubber. With grave determination, she was the first to take a sailboat up the Columbia River. My frayed brown leather scrapbooks are testament to the news reports of taking out a few power lines with her mast! Illness took her from me when I was only two, but my father carried on the passion they had shared for the wind among our various sailing vessels. His last sleek white twenty-eight-foot sloop, he proudly named *Toy Boat Toy Boat Toy Boat*, which he had painted on her stern in bright red. When the attendants at the Chittenden Locks, the passage between Lake Washington and Puget Sound, had to verify the vessel's name to pass through, he tried to trip them up.

He grinned sheepishly as he held the radio microphone to his lips. "Requesting permission to enter," he'd call.

"Vessel name?" they'd reply dryly.

His eyes would crinkle at the corners as he winked at me, while he offered his well-rehearsed answer and waited for them to repeat it. There was a lengthy pause. They always copped out, answering curtly, "*Toy Boat*, proceed." Chickens.

I learned early that being at the helm didn't always mean there was a direct route to my destination. Tacking and jibing, reading the telltales to interpret the whims of the wind, became a foretaste of the path of my life. At times I had the lines hauled in so close, and was heeled over so far, the green water in the portholes made me think

WORK AT SEA, SEE THE WORLD: AN INSIDER'S SECRETS TO THE WORKING LIFE ON A CRUISE SHIP

maybe I'd pushed my ambitions too far and I was destined to capsize. Other times I found that jibing to put the wind at my back had me running before it, straightening me up and putting me on flat water. I found myself speeding along without a care, with a destination clearly in sight. I have tacked this way and that, adapting to the winds that blew at the time. But somehow, with the Grace of God, I managed to find my way through both the gales and the calms. But no matter where I went, the salt water of the oceans in which I swam off that sloop, and the ocean spray that showered over me onboard may be washed off, but would never dry. Instead, it seems to have seeped into my blood. I cannot bear the thought of living anywhere without sight of water.

But now, as much as I still love to sail, I find I am content to let others manage the helm and the hard work of the mechanics and the navigation. The courses plotted on much-bigger boats take me to places I have never known, across oceans and seas, to the far reaches of the earth. I have found a way to enjoy the freedom to explore the expansive worldwide destinations that were once far beyond the reach of my tiny sails. For me, a life at sea also brings with it an international family of characters, each with multiple skills and talents with which to share new horizons. But I have to wonder what my mother would have thought about my graduation from tiny sailing boats to the giant, megaton, ocean-going vessels that now carry me on strange and exciting journeys.

My life's adventures have been expanded to include the whole world by working on a cruise ship.

CHAPTER 1

This Is Not Just a Regular Job!

A cruise ship, you say? What? And you may well ask the following questions. Why would I want to live on the ocean? Would I get seasick? What job could I do? Can I do there what I do on land? Could I actually get to visit exotic destinations and get paid for it? Might I actually consider this as a possible career option? In the following chapters, you will find answers to these questions and get a taste of the world of life onboard as a crewmember. For me, the answer came in the form of my dream job, which was to sing in a jazz band. I got paid to see the world, could do what I love every night, and managed to keep that salt water flowing in my veins.

  The lure of the ocean has haunted man since they learned how to strap logs together to make a raft. Obviously we have come a *long* way from those days to where an entire city will float! If the sea fever has gotten ahold of you, you may be wondering, can one actually get paid to use your particular job skills and see the world on one of these monster vessels? Generally prime ages of applicants range from nineteen to fifty-something (see chapter 23 for the over forties). So grab your passport; here we go.

  Okay, so why would anybody in their right mind leave perfectly solid ground to go to sea? For those who grew up landlocked, the thought of living on the ocean may be daunting. "But I can't swim!" you say. No worries, you won't have to, and you won't be alone where that skill is concerned. But it certainly helps when you find yourself with the opportunity to enjoy exotic beaches in your travels. This endeavor may be a chance to embrace a new and exciting way of life. Floating on the massive oceans of the world that occupy over 70 percent of the planet, you understand the anxiety of the ancient mariners. That flat horizon convinced them that there was an edge to the world and to sail too far would cause them to fall off into oblivion. Obviously proven wrong by some brave sailors, the hazards are not in its flatness but in its unpredictableness.

Sailors must respect the power of Mother Nature and are forced to adapt to her whims. Away from the lights and congestion of a city, you have to be amazed at the magnificent grandeur of the universe as you stand on the deck on a clear night, feeling the warm breeze on your skin, catching the salty scent of the ocean, hearing the lapping of the waves on the ship's hull, and being overwhelmed by the infinite mass of diamonds aglow in the velvet dome above. The waves shift and morph constantly and are shaped by the currents, the tides, and the winds. You marvel at the sea animals with which you share this planet, as the sleek albatross spreads her wings to ride the wind currents above or watch seagulls greedily dive into your wake in search of food. Depending on where you sail, you may even see massive whales breaching above the surface, lazy sea lions lounging on frozen icebergs or basking on stretches of warm beaches.

Life itself is so like the ocean, unpredictable and often intimidating. In learning to adapt to those changes in life, you can't help but gain a new perspective on yourself, your potential, and your place in the world. Winds may change and tides may turn, but you emerge from the fog of childhood and grow to find your way, and those winds of change may blow you in a new and exciting direction. To paraphrase Robert Frost, taking that alternative chosen path "makes all the difference." You learn to weather the storms and adapt to the new directions of the wind. One of my favorite lines from Shakespeare is Romeo's prayer, "*May He, that hath the steerage of my course, direct my sail!*"

So let's look at how this works. Gone are the days of being at the whim of the wind by sail, and the sophisticated navigational and atmospheric instruments along with the excessive power built into today's vessels have all but eliminated the deadliest hazards once associated with sailing the oceans. There are now basically two types of passenger-friendly ocean-going vessels, but the differences are becoming negligible in today's cruise-oriented world.

1. *Ocean liners* originally were sleek designs typically built for open-ocean crossings, with high speeds and dedicated timeline itineraries. An aquadynamic hull design built of strong steel is intended to move people and/or products from one place to another on fixed and repeated routes, and withstand the extremes of transatlantic crossings from one port to another (think New York to London). Ocean liners were even used in WWII to transport troops because of their speed and maneuverability. These vessels have a longer bow than other ships and a higher bridge and lifeboat decks. Some are now built to serve double duty with cruise ship-type facilities and itineraries that may include more tourist-related stops and more relaxed timelines.

Cunard's *Queen Mary 2*

2. *Cruise ships* are designed to be floating resorts with numerous ports of call built into the itinerary. Group activities and

shore excursions expand the opportunities for adventure, and the larger ships have become a destination in themselves, providing fun all the way; think bumper cars, wind-tunnel sky-diving, rock climbing, laser tag, giant multideck slides, water parks, zip lines, miniature golf, and simulated surfing! Some are so big you are not even aware you are floating. A cruise vacation has become synonymous with luxury and comfort. As such, there is a large proportion of the working budget and personnel devoted to musical entertainment and amusements such as bands, Broadway/West End productions, ice shows, and aqua shows. Most companies have several brands under their corporate umbrella. Total worldwide ocean cruise capacity as of 2021 included over 50 cruise lines representing 323 ships worldwide, serving more than 581,000 guests. Capacity is expected to increase by one third by 2025. These numbers are constantly changing as sailing capacities fluctuate, vessels change owners, older ones may be scrapped, and newer and bigger ones are constantly being built.

Royal Caribbean's *Allure of the Seas*

3. Just to round out the job options, for smaller bodies of water, alternative positions can be found on the extensive

fleet of over 500 river cruise boats from Silversea, Seabourn, SeaDream, CroisiEurope, Windstar, and Viking River Cruises among others. These boats generally carry between 100 and 300 guests each. They have extensive itineraries for rivers in both Europe and the United States. However, given their small size and limited space, generally entertainment may be provided by local performers brought onboard at the various ports. These river-oriented companies can generally be approached directly online for openings for the limited availability of guest service-oriented positions.

Ocean-wise, these are the major corporate conglomerates that presently rule the seas:

Cruise Company	Number of Ships	Passenger Capacity
Carnival Corporation		
Carnival	25	71,300
Costa	11	50,713
Princess	14	42,000
AIDA	13	29,300

Holland America	11	25,900
P&O UK	6	18,600
P&O AU	3	8,200
Cunard	3	6,700
Seabourn	5	1,950
Royal Caribbean Group		
RCI	27	84,700
Celebrity	13	25,500
Azamara	3	2,100
TUI	6	14,900
Silversea	6	4,916
Norwegian Cruise Lines		
NCL	16	46,600
Oceana	6	5,200
Regent	4	2,600
Others		
MSC	15	44,600
Disney	4	8,500
Star	5	8,500
Pullmantur	4	7,600
Dream Cruises	2	6,800
Hurtigruten	6	6,700
Viking	5	4,700
Celestyal Cruises	4	4,400
Viking Ocean	6	5,580
Virgin	1	2,770
Crystal Cruises	2	1,992

Other Smaller Companies
American Cruise Lines
Bahamas Paradise Cruise Line
Celestyal Cruises
Cruise and Maritime Voyages
Fred Olsen Cruise Lines
Jalesh Cruises
Marella Cruises
Paul Gauguin Cruises
Ponant Cruises
Ritz-Carlton Yacht Collection
Saga Cruises
SeaDream Yacht Club
Scenic Luxury Cruises
Windstar Cruises

Quantities and ownership information as of 2020. Some may have been sold or scrapped, and new ones built and added to the fleets. Numbers subject to change.

The next chapter will outline many of the numerous job positions onboard. For access to hiring partners, see information in the appendix. If traveling is not your preference, there are thousands of positions needed shoreside or on tropical islands to support the operations of the ships. Check the job listings as appropriate for locations and opportunities.

CHAPTER 2

Give It a Try

Best Advice: Try It First

As a majority of the employment opportunities will be found on cruise ships, they will be the focus of what's to follow. If you have never been on a cruise, try one out. So many ships offer inexpensive vacations, even a short three-day weekend getaway. Go see what all the fuss is about. It helps if you live near a major coastal port city where cruise ship itineraries begin, but take a plane or drive if you must. Cruising has the advantage of being an all-inclusive adventure which can bundle the costs of airfare to the departure port, hotel accommodations prior to the cruise, transportation to the ship, food, and a pleasant stateroom. Size and features vary with the price, and cabins located midship and on lower decks are the most stable and often the least expensive. You will meet people from other parts of the country or the world. Get onboard, unpack into your tiny closet, and let your "hotel" move from place to place. No schlepping bags from cab to hotel over and over, trying to find out where to eat at your destination, struggling with language barriers, exchanging currencies, or paying for taxis, etc. You can do all these things, if you so choose, in your ports of call, but you don't have to! You get a taste of various countries should you choose to return for a longer stay. You have the same bed every night, with clean sheets, and a crazy creative towel animal to greet you and all the food you can eat!

WORK AT SEA, SEE THE WORLD: AN INSIDER'S SECRETS TO THE WORKING LIFE ON A CRUISE SHIP

The ships typically sail at night, and you arrive at a new port in the morning so you can explore ashore. Planned excursions focus on local highlights, or you can investigate the town on your own. When in transit between ports, enjoy a relaxing day at sea where you can participate in a plethora of activities and amusements, or do absolutely nothing if you so choose! Nap in the sun on the pool deck, curl up with a book on a comfy couch in a quiet lounge, or sit on your stateroom balcony and enjoy the fresh air and magnificent scenery. Try your hand at the casino or play bingo. Taking a cruise as a guest would give you a clue as to whether this is a world in which you could live for an extended period. Enjoy the free entertainment in lounges and showrooms while you scope out the potential job options. The following information will give you a clue as to what goes on below decks and the differences in guest versus crew accommodations. Chat with crewmembers that represent an area of interest for you and get their input on life onboard. They're not allowed to discuss salaries, and of course, your particular skills and experience will dictate yours, should you decide to pursue a role in the job market. If you have any concerns about the motion of the ocean, the larger ships and routes that stay closer to coastlines tend to be more stable on the water.

The largest source market for cruise passengers was the United States in 2016, with 11.52 million passengers. In comparison, the number of passengers from the second and third largest source markets, China and Germany, amounted to just 2.1 and 2.02 million passengers respectively. In 2019, the ships hosted about thirty million guests, and numbers have fluctuated in the years following due to the pandemic and world events. The leading international travel destination for US travelers year-round (as forecast by Travel Leaders Group agents) was for the Caribbean cruises. The most popular US domestic cruise destination was Alaska, which is seasonal. Passenger capacity in the Asian markets was over 4 million in 2019. Most of the ports of call depend heavily on the tourist industry to support their economy, so whether it is a mainland city or an island, the residents count on the ships to bring them paying customers for their products and services, and tourism is most often their primary (or only) industry. Some ships cater to citizens of specific countries and hence carry a clientele that predominantly speak the relevant language (Spanish, Chinese, German, etc.), even though the language requirement for all crew is fluency in English.

As of 2022, the five largest ships in the world by gross tonnage are part of the Royal Caribbean fleet: the *Wonder of the Seas* and the *Symphony of the Seas* (at 228,000 gross tons), the *Harmony of the Seas* (227,000 gross tons), and the *Allure* and the *Oasis of the Seas* (both at 225,282 gross tons). More ships are always under construction as well, so the maximum size is yet to come, but the Royal Caribbean *Icon of the Seas* (January 2024) weighs in at 250,800 gross tons with 2350 crewmembers and 7600 guests (so, lots of employment options!) next smaller are Carnival's *Celebration* and *Mardi Gras* at 184,000 gross tons. Just to give some scale to these huge numbers, the *Titanic* was 46,000 gross tons. Each company's vessels have their own advantages/disadvantages, so they are each unique. The smaller classes of cruise ships are about 74,000 gross tons with about 2,000 guests. Currently the biggest carries 6,680 guests, plus 2,200 crew. Routes and amenities are all different. Peruse the companies' websites for details. Never confuse a boat with a ship. You can put a boat on a ship (think lifeboat), but you can't put a ship on a boat!

The cruise industry is projected to boast $57 billion in revenue by 2027 and, as of 2020, had already hosted over thirty-two million guests. Some landlubbers may cast a disparaging eye, but the benefits of this business are tremendously widespread. The industry supports innumerable jobs including transportation companies, dockworkers, numerous and varied suppliers of food, clothing, retail merchandise, and shop sundries, not to mention the hundreds of thousands of crew jobs supporting innumerable workers and their families. And the benefits extend to the massive influx of revenue brought to the travel destinations. The 2020 halting of cruise traffic due to the COVID-19 pandemic resulted in devastating effects from the complete halting of cruise travel for ships worldwide, which lasted nearly a year and took several more to recover.

Major Considerations

A typical ship's crew contract can last generally four to nine months, variable by position and rank. Marine officers of rank are more typically on a ten-week-on, ten-week-off schedule. But those positions are much fewer than the typical jobs onboard. Ideally this life most easily suits one who is single, with minimal land-based obligations, but many others rely on the income to support their families back in their countries. Not every relationship can withstand this sort of separation, hence this adventure does not suit everyone. There are sacrifices and other elements to consider:

1. This is life on a moving ship. Not everyone is comfortable with the motion of the ocean. Be aware that some jobs require a predominantly indoor lifestyle. Yes, there are open decks and ports to explore, but much of your work

time may be spent inside, depending on position. Ships are generally built with advanced and efficient ventilation systems, and spaces are cleaned and sanitized regularly. It is encouraged (and essential) to wash hands at every opportunity and utilize the sanitizer stations found everywhere. If you are wise and sensible, there should be no problems. Should a need arise, there is a full-time medical staff on hand for any situation. Should a specialist or particular equipment be required in a medical emergency, you would be dispatched immediately to an appropriate hospital at the nearest port for further treatment. As a crew member, the cost of all this is covered under your employment contract. Should you prefer a land-based job, there are also opportunities with corporate headquarters. Many companies also have their own private tropical islands, usually in sunny climates, that need maintenance and attendants if you prefer more of an outdoor lifestyle with land beneath your feet.

2. Minimal communication with friends and family can be a challenge. Ship-to-shore calling cards are available onboard, but cell service can be pricey (see notes on carriers). Depending on the company, Wi-Fi is usually charged by time used. FaceTime, Skype, and Zoom that require Wi-Fi are sometimes either slow, inconvenient, or expensive; and there are more alternatives being developed for better communication (WhatsApp, Telegram, etc.). There are usually crew-rate Internet packages available for purchase onboard at reduced rates to help facilitate communications.

3. Accommodations are small, often windowless, perhaps shared with a stranger (or more than one) who may be from another country. Some might have unusual habits (some like to sleep in the nude—maybe that's you!). The walls are generally magnetic, however, and you can bring along photos to "home" it up with souvenir magnets.

4. Food is good and abundant but rather redundant in menu options. Multiple ethnicities must be accommodated, so

usually *lots* of rice, curry, Indonesian, East Indian, and Filipino food. The menu choices can be a challenge if you are vegan or have allergies; although crew chefs are usually accommodating. You learn to be creative with what you have available. Sometimes augmentation from port sources may be available for your personal snacks.
5. There is a defined military hierarchy, lots of rules, and strict bosses, with everyone's safety as a priority. But just mind your P's and Q's, be cooperative and respectful, and you'll be okay. It is essential that everyone can rely on all others using common sense and behaving responsibly.
6. Schedules can be erratic in terms of ship duties and emergency-preparedness exercises. Being flexible at all times is important. There are no weekends or days off, and calling in sick is not an option unless it's essential, debilitating, or contagious.

So why would anybody put themselves through a life like this?

1. A steady direct-deposit paycheck for four to nine months. Nothing to sneeze at.
2. No overhead: room, food, health insurance, air and ground transportation to/from ship anywhere in the world all paid for. Sweet.
3. Crew parties. Once you do get to know those with whom you work/live, you may find you have much in common and develop friendships with people from other countries. The Human Resources Department is keenly aware of the need to make living together as pleasant as possible. Any country's holidays are always a reason to celebrate. In the evenings, there is a crew bar providing inexpensive drinks, and there is always music, be it a DJ, karaoke, or live playing from fellow crew members. If you are single, it is not uncommon to find close relationships and even potential long-term commitments among your fellow crew members.

4. You travel to amazing places in the world, some of which you may have never known existed. Vanuatu, Bora Bora, or Mystery Island, anyone? Or others with which you may be familiar: Venice, Barcelona, Sydney, etc. You may even visit these places several times, depending on your itinerary. You'll find your favorite haunts, and the whole planet will become your home. A world that once seemed so huge will become a familiar part of your experience.
5. Crew excursions. Crew may be allowed to use dedicated private beaches or access local boat trips, etc. Bicycles may be available onboard to help you explore. Or if you don't mind accompanying guests, some companies offer a chance to be an excursion escort. As a liaison between the ship and the local tour guides, you go along to help out and complete a short report on any tour particulars. Or you can explore the ports on your own (always advisable to go with friends). Just be sure to make it back at least an hour before sailing!

Okay, I hear you asking, "Can I make any money at this game?" Well, yes. Remember that the joy in life is about the journey. It will take some self-assessment about your lifestyle tolerances under unusual circumstances, but just believe that it is indeed possible. If you play your cards right, you can support yourself, a family, or build a retirement nest egg and have some fun in the bargain. But there are rules (don't you just hate it when there's a catch?). Pay scale will depend on the company, the job, your particular skills and experience, and possibly your home country's economy. Your hiring contact will narrow down the particulars.

Just to be fair, before we get into more reasons *why*, let's take a quick look at *why not*:

1. Yes, there is no denying that you are an employee in a massive corporation: an important and vital cog in a very large wheel. But you are the only one doing your particular job, and you are crucial.

2. Cruise ships have never been noted for their healthy cuisine. Crew chefs will try to accommodate particular dietary requirements, but they are cooking tens of thousands of meals every day. There is always plenty of food, just maybe not always to your exact taste. You can choose to expand your horizons (dahl or fish heads, anyone?). Staff are open to suggestions, but you need to be flexible and maybe creative with what is offered. If you're a vegan, there will be challenges.
3. The opportunity for your own private space may be limited. Cabins are small, and you literally have to go outside to change your mind!
4. The crew bar tends to facilitate way too much alcohol and cigarettes, so beware. Allowed alcohol consumption is limited, but easy availability can make it tempting.
5. Watch out, there will be even the slightest excuse for a party at every opportunity.
6. Work schedules will vary tremendously between departments, positions, and companies. But generally, as mentioned, there will be no official days off and no weekends. But there will indeed be free time. Maritime law regulates the maximum amount of work hours and the mandatory rest hours (see details in the appendix). The excitement of exploring foreign ports is immeasurable and crew members are encouraged to take advantage of the port opportunities whenever schedules allow.

CHAPTER 3

How to Get the Job

There are numerous roles to be played onboard, and each has their own requirements. Some departments hire several people for one specific job, and for others, there is only one job occasionally up for grabs. The ship is indeed a floating city, and many of the jobs you may hold on land might also apply to this unique environment. But there are specific roles and a set of allotted crew cabins for each position. If you are qualified or interested in any of the positions listed below, you can start with the website:

http://www.allcruisejobs.com*.*

Here you can find a listing of job openings available, get more specific details on what each job entails, what they are looking for in candidates, or get assistance with résumés and applications. You may also find listings on the company websites of any of the cruise lines in which you are interested (see the appendix for direct contact and application information).

You may also find a variety of hiring partners that specialize in different department's fulfillment at ***https://cruisejobdirectory.com****.* The primary requirement in all cases is *fluency in the English language*, required by maritime law worldwide. In addition, some companies cater to guests of a particular country, and additional fluency in the language of the sailing region will be preferred (Germans, Italians, Chinese, etc.), especially if you are in a position where direct guest interaction is required. If you have experience or interest in any of these positions, you very well may be chosen for one of these treasured jobs. Let the adventure begin!

EXECUTIVE MANAGEMENT: *Senior positions requiring extensive training. If you're qualified for these, you already know who you are. Descriptions below in case one of them becomes your boss:*

    Captain/master
    Staff captain
    Hotel manager/hotel director
    Assistant hotel manager
    Chief engineer
    Chief purser
    Cruise director
    Food and beverage manager
    Sanitation officer

HOUSEKEEPING DEPARTMENT: *all positions involved with hotel operations*

    Executive housekeeper
    Assistant housekeeper
    Cabin steward/stewardess
    Hotel utility/cleaner
    Laundry staff
    Deck steward/pool attendant
    Bell person
    Tailor
    Florist

GALLEY: *responsible for food preparation for guests and crew*

    Executive chef de cuisine
    Executive sous chef
    Chef de cuisine
    Junior sous chef
    Chef de partie

Cook/commis de cuisine

Pastry:

Executive pastry chef
Sous chef pastry
Demi chef de partie pastry
Commis de cuisine pastry

Bakery:

Chief baker
Chef de partie baker
Commis de cuisine baker

Other:

Butcher
Galley utility
Dishwasher

RESTAURANTS: *requiring excellent guest-service skills in providing food and drinks*

Food and beverage manager
Assistant food and beverage manager
Restaurant manager
Maître d' hotel
Waiter/waitress
Restaurant host/hostess

BEVERAGE: *serving hot/cold (alcoholic and nonalcoholic) drinks in bars, cafés, and restaurants*

Bar manager
Bartender

Sommelier/wine steward
Bar waiter/waitress
Barista

PROVISIONS: *managing food and supplies for guests and crew*

Hotel controller
Provisions master
Assistant storekeeper

DECK JOBS: *deck department officers and crew, responsible for smooth operation of the ship*

First officer/first mate
Second officer
Third officer
Environmental officer
Chief communication/radio officer
Deck cadet

Safety/security:

Chief officer safety
Security officer
Security guard

DECK RATING: *Seaman's Book required, and you already know if you're qualified.*

Bosun
Able seaman
Ordinary seaman
Carpenter/joiner
Upholsterer

PHOTOGRAPHY: *Take pictures of passengers during embarkation, parties, dinners, etc. Must be extroverted, sales-focused people, able to sell their service to the guests, and develop films, process pictures, manage digital media, set up shoots, and sell photos and equipment to passengers.*

    Photo manager
    Assistant photo manager
    Photographer
    Video operator/videographer

SHORE EXCURSIONS: *Offering short trips and excursions on land. Manager is responsible for supervising excursion staff, as well as promotion and arrangement of excursions.*

    Shore excursion manager
    Assistant shore excursion manager
    Shore excursion staff
    Port and shopping guide

MEDICAL: *Doctors and nurses are on call at all times; they perform routine and emergency care to passengers and crew members. Some ships also have dentists.*

    Doctor
    Nurse

SPORTS AND FITNESS: *supervision of a variety of sports and fitness activities including surfing, snorkeling, scuba diving, swimming, golf, yoga, Pilates, indoor skydiving, gym use, and wall climbing.*

    Fitness instructor/personal trainer
    Yoga/Pilates teacher
    Sports staff
    Lifeguard
    Some ships have scuba diving instruction or iFLY.

WORK AT SEA, SEE THE WORLD: AN INSIDER'S SECRETS TO THE WORKING LIFE ON A CRUISE SHIP

CASINO: *casinos are often operated by concessionaires; staff is responsible for smooth operation of casino games and slot machines.*

> Casino manager
> Assistant casino manager
> Pit boss
> Casino dealers
> Casino cashier
> Slot technician

IT/COMPUTER TECH: *managing complex information technology to administer and maintain both hardware and software.*

> Systems manager
> Computer technician

ENGINE AND TECHNICAL: *Engine department crew are responsible for smooth operation of the ship. All employees must hold correct maritime qualifications.*

> Chief engineer
> Staff chief engineer
> First engineer
> Second engineer
> Third engineer
> Engine cadet

Electrotechnical:

> Chief electrician
> First electrician
> Electrician
> Electrotechnical officers

Other:

> Ventilation/refrigeration officer
> Hotel maintenance manager
> Waste disposal staff
> Engine storekeeper
> Motorman
> Plumber

GUEST SERVICES: *passenger service roles requiring excellent customer service skills; fluency in several languages is often required, and exceptional computer skills.*

> Guest services manager
> Guest services officer
> Receptionist/concierge
> Director of diversity and inclusion
> Night auditor
> International host/hostess (fluency in at least four languages)
> Future cruise consultant
> Butler/genie
> Desktop publisher/printer

RETAIL: *most retail outlets are run by concessionaires; typically selling cruise line's merchandise, perfumes, high-end jewelry, fashion accessories, handbags, and watches.*

> Shop manager
> Assistant shop manager
> Retail salesperson
> Art auctioneer
> Jewelry specialist
> Watch specialist

NEXT CRUISE SALES: *promotion of future cruise bookings for onboard guests.*

    Cruise sales manager
    Salesperson

SPA/BEAUTY: *providing a range of services including hairstyling, massages, beauty treatments. Most regulated by Steiner Leisure Ltd. which may require training in either London or Philippines.*

    Spa manager
    Spa attendant/receptionist
    Beautician
    Hairstylist
    Massage therapist
    Nail technician
    Acupuncturist
    Medispa facial treatment doctor

CHILDCARE: *youth counselors, childcare staff and childcare supervisors responsible for entertaining and caring of children.*

    Youth counselor
    Nannies

ENTERTAINMENT: *anything related to passenger entertainment, including artistic performances, competitions, and onboard TV broadcasting.*

    Cruise director
    Assistant cruise director/activities manager
    Stage manager
    Stage staff
    Theatrical rigger
    Light technician
    Sound technician

Broadcast technician
Desktop publisher
Cruise staff
Host/hostess
Lecturer
Musician (solo performer or ensemble group. See my book
   Notes That Float for details and specifics)
Singer
Dancer (chorus or specialty)
Musical theater actors
Aerialist
Disc jockey
Ballroom dancer*
Figure skater*
High-diver*
Platform/springboard diver*
Synchronized swimmer*
Slack-line performer*
High-wire performer*
(*only for some ships)

ADMINISTRATION: *responsible for various administrative tasks such as accounting, immigration issues, document handling, office work, crew assistance, etc.*

Chief purser
First purser
Crew purser
Accountant
Marketing and revenue manager
Ship's secretary

The corporate ladder is headed by the king of your conglomerate company, then there are the numerous layers of corporate royalty below leading to your captain, and he/she is the boss of your ship. Onboard life is built on a very military hierarchy. The ship officers have stripes on their epaulets and coat sleeves, just like in the military, and they are in charge. They have earned those stripes! If you so desire, you, too, could work toward wearing those bars as well. Some companies choose to keep the ranks less obvious, so you may not be clued in to the fact that you are speaking directly to the captain or the hotel manager, so watch what you say!

Here is a brief list of the major boss positions:

- ***The captain*** is ultimately the Big Cheese in charge and is responsible for the safety and well-being of his ship, its passengers, and crew. He or she has many years of experience in all aspects of navigation, management, operations, and mechanics and is the final authority on all ship issues but still has to answer to the corporate big wigs.
- ***The staff captain*** is the Second Banana. This role is to ensure the carrying out of the captain's orders and, in an emergency, is trained to take over or relieve the captain. They help run the ship and work with all the department heads (the executive committee) to maintain safety, oversee the emergency plan, handle matters of misconduct from guests or crew (yes, you!), supervise the deck maintenance and other ship operations, and work closely with the captain and other officers on all pertinent issues.
- ***The chief engineer*** is the boss of anything related to the actual mechanics of running the ship, including the engineers, carpenters, electricians, plumbers, and deckhands; also schedules and supervises the fueling, maintenance, etc.
- ***The hotel director*** manages the cabin attendants, cleaning crew, guest services agents, and the entertainment division. Laundry services come under their direction, as well as provisions management and hotel supplies and maintenance.
- ***The food and beverage manager*** is responsible for all the dining rooms' operations, chefs, galleys, food-preparation workers, waitstaff, provision systems, and supplies.
- ***Chief officer safety*** is (duh!) in charge of the safety of everyone onboard. He supervises his training officers and

the security team. *Never* mess with this guy. He can boot you off at a moment's notice if you endanger anyone—anything—or disrespect him/her or the safety team.
- ***The safety officer*** is in charge of trainings and has a lot of power. If you do not seem able to grasp the severity and details of these trainings (fire safety, basic medical assistance, crowd control, etc.) and are not fluent in English, you could be sent home.
- ***The cruise director*** supervises the entire entertainment department and guest activities. Also he/she manages drill announcements, guest embarkation, all onboard events, disembarkation, etc. Often they record a daily televised information show for the guests. They supervise a large team and control all the guest-activity schedules, coordinating with *all* other departments. Lots of meetings involved, staying up very late, getting up very early.
- ***The activities manager*** works directly with the cruise director to manage onboard guests' activities including games, trivia, etc.
- ***The production manager(s)*** of the theater(s) work with the cruise director to schedule and manage the entertainment facilities. They manage the stage staff, as well as the sound and light technicians, and relevant riggers of the various performance venues.
- ***The music director*** performs as the leader of the orchestra and manages the performance schedule of all the bands and performers among other music-related duties. (See my book *Notes that Float* for specific details on musical occupations and band/performer requirements.)
- ***The human resources manager*** and staff will become your best friends. This team assists in the smooth cooperation of the crew. They manage cabin assignments, receive mail, issue your safety emergency card and your cabin key (and fix it if you ruin one), create your crew identification card, manage crew shore excursions, and orchestrate harmonious living accommodations, handling any crew issues.

- ***The financial officer*** is the guy in charge of the money (sometimes referred to as the purser). Once you have your crew ID card, you may have to put some money into your onboard account to purchase from the slop chest (the crew store) or gift shops, etc., or have it linked to a credit card to cover your expenses. Using your OceanPay card or Salary@ Sea may be an option, depending on the ship's system, allowing expenses to be deducted from your paycheck.
- ***Other***: The casino, photo department, the shops onboard (jewelry, souvenirs, clothing, sundries, etc.), shore excursions, cruise sales, and art gallery each have their own independent managerial operations who mostly report to the hotel director, but the workers there are still crew and participate in training, drills, and most onboard operational functions.

So did you find a post that interests you? The following chapters will provide some general crew information regarding how to prepare for leaving, signing on, trainings required, living arrangements, signing off, etc. There may be changes in the post-2020 world, and differences regarding prerequisites, rank, position, and privileges for different cruise lines. For more details, refer to actual online job postings. For interacting with the officers, *respect the office and respect the person*, and all will go well.

The information that follows will be relevant to *all new-hire crew*, regardless of department. You will find some amusing comments from crew of various companies and positions. Whatever your job onboard, you will find a new family of international characters that will provide a new adventure and an expanded perspective on the world. Regardless of the job for which you are hired, your primary job is *safety* of all onboard. This life is not for everyone, but it is guaranteed to open your mind. Despite some long working hours, the companies go out of their way to provide a crew experience that is fun, safe, and positive. Most crews are comprised of members from sixty to ninety different countries, all living under the same roof and obliged to get along, often accomplishing more efficient relationships than those at the United Nations. You will find members of various ethnicities, religions, traditions, habits, and languages. Some ships even have a position entitled Director of Diversity and Tolerance. But joining this unique family requires not just toleration of differences but an attitude of celebration of distinctions. We were not all born into equal circumstances, but we are all allowed equal opportunity. Life constantly brings us to crossroads, and Robert Frost was onto something when he *"took the one less traveled by, and that has made all the difference."* Sometimes the road we need is not in the woods but a new path to adventure that could be found on the sea. Welcome to the vast and varied outside world; get ready for the ride of your life!

Here's just a small sampling of some of the countries from which I have personally encountered fellow crew members:

    Argentina
    Australia
    Belarus
    Brazil
    Bulgaria
    Canada
    China
    Columbia
    Costa Rica
    Croatia
    Dominican Republic
    El Salvador
    France
    Greece
    Haiti
    Honduras
    India
    Italy
    Jamaica
    Japan
    Korea
    Kenya

Macedonia
Montenegro
Mexico
New Zealand
Norway
Peru
Philippines
Portugal
Romania
Russia
Serbia
South Africa
Spain
Sweden
Turkey
Ukraine
United Kingdom
United States

You will make friends with fellow crew members from many countries. Get ready for the challenges of interacting in so many ways. Have you got what it takes? Review the following list to see. Let the adventure continue onboard.

CHAPTER 4

What You Need to Know About Living Onboard

The world is a book, and those who do not travel read only one page.

—Saint Augustine

Here are some things of which you have to be aware. Ship life involves a mixture of nationalities, ages, and ranges of experience. There are basic requirements that apply to anyone seeking ship work.

1. *No illegal drugs of any kind*—This is a **zero**-tolerance situation. No potheads or alternative/ illegal "medicinal" choices. They may be legit back home, but absolutely not at sea. If you try to sneak them aboard, be prepared to be busted and put off at the next port, returning home at your own expense or even jailed in a foreign country. Trust me, they're on to you, and the penalties can be severe and life changing. Violations will be serious and have extensive repercussions.
2. *A clean record*—If you have any criminal activity on your record, this may disqualify you right off the bat. Period.

You will be required to provide a background check before you are accepted.

3. *Physical fitness*—Strength and agility are constantly required. Beyond schlepping your luggage, there is a lot of walking, steep metal crew stairs, some excessively heavy doors, and you may find yourself sleeping on the upper level of a bunk bed on a moving ship. A very thorough medical report will be required. Ability to enact safety duties will require agility and fitness.

4. *Compatibility*—Living in close quarters requires adapting to others' habits. Basic respect and consideration for one another is key. Proper personal hygiene and tidiness are essential. You live in a *very* small space, possibly with strangers. Respect others' belongings. Be courteous and tolerant of others. *Please* can more easily resolve a situation over anger. If issues persist, the department head, the human resources manager, or the staff captain can help. But realize you must be able to cooperate well with others, both at work and at rest. Headphones/earbuds, sleep mask, and earplugs are often vital tools to maintain peace and sanity.

5. *Coachability*—You are responsible for the safety of guests and fellow crew members. Eighty hours of training are required that cover various aspects of ship safety. I'll say it again—the primary requirement, the maritime standard worldwide, for any portion of ship life is fluency in speaking, reading, and understanding English, and you must be physically able to handle your assigned tasks. Pay attention to the details of training and embrace the responsibility associated therewith.

6. *Commitment*—Regardless of your country of origin, your decision to accept the job means that wherever you are sent in the world, if you are allowed shore leave, you promise to return to the ship as required. To "jump ship" has dire and extensive penalties and ongoing consequences. Worldwide visas may be denied for both you and any member of your

family indefinitely. In this high-tech world, you cannot *disappear*. You bear much responsibility for both your future and that of others.

Okay, all that said, are you still game? You will find in the following chapters the logistics of how to apply for the job. You will find information on how to manage life that's left at home, how to get where you're going, what will be required onboard, and a bit of a portrait of how life will roll should you choose to accept this challenge. Just as in sailing, the course in life is rarely a straight line, and sometimes you just have to trust that you have correctly read the wind that's steering your boat in the right direction. Take the helm and know that regardless of the tacks you have to make, the journey will be worth it and the destination rewarding.

> *One life on this earth is all that we get, whether it is enough or not enough, and the obvious conclusion would seem to be that at the very least we are fools if we do not live it as fully and bravely and beautifully as we can.*
>
> —Frederick Buechner

CHAPTER 5

So You Got the Job! Now What?

So are you game to check it out? For hiring partners to help you secure the gig, again, see the website *http://www.allcruise jobs.com*. The appendix lists several other avenues of contact to enable your search. It may take some patience to get connected with the right contact for the correct position for you. The companies receive a tremendous number of applications, so it may take a while. Don't give up your day job until you get a confirmation. There will usually be at least a month advance notice, so just hang in there. Once you get the offer, they realize there is time necessary to complete the required background checks and completed medical forms before a contract can be finalized. The notice (usually by e-mail) that you will receive from your company or agency contact will say, in essence, "This is what we've got available. Do you want it?" The only details they may give are the name of the cruise company, the ship, the position, the contract dates of start/end, and the embarkation location.

Once you accept the offer, your first order of business is to be sure you have *a valid passport.* In the United States, all the information to get one into process can be found at *http://www.usa.gov* or at *http://www.usps.com.* The latter will take you to the post office site where you can get information on how to get a passport photo and all the forms required for submission. This piece of documentation is *crucial* for travel anywhere in the world. If you already have one, check that there are at least six months valid past the end of the expected contract period. Your country's requirements may be different, so check with your government agency for where you need to go and what you need to do to get this started or renew it. If working in United States waters, depending on your country, you may also need to obtain an I-95 form or a Seaman's Book, which can be obtained once onboard.

Second priority is to make necessary appointments to complete the medical report requirements. There may be specific locations in your town or country that must be utilized to comply with the company's requirements. This will involve a complete physical, including a blood test, chest x-ray, eyesight assessment, mobility check, and statement of general health. This is the most important document to assure acceptance onboard. It must be completed in English, so you may need to download an extra set of forms in case it needs to be translated by a medical representative; be sure they are all signed correctly by the doctors! Confirm any medication prescriptions as necessary.

Third priority is to check your cell phone plan. Once you know where you are headed, check with your carrier to determine whether you are on the right plan for your destination. You will want to rely on this little device for contact with your homies. Sometimes an alternative is to get a SIM card for your destination country if it's consistent, or you may find you're better off to change carriers. Find out their accessibility and adjust as necessary. Avoid roaming. Ship-to-shore calls can also be made with a calling card available onboard.

Fourth, you will be required to get a verification of a satisfactory background check. This is usually accomplished online by a recommended site. In the US, one source is *http://www.criminalrecords.us.org*, but check with your company for their specific requirements.

Okay, those are the four essential elements to be sure you have either in hand, or in the works, before you start even thinking about taking the next step. Some companies will have you submit a copy of your passport, the completed background check, and the medical forms before they finalize your contract details or issue any travel documents. Once job acceptance is confirmed, it's time to rearrange your life. So you've got the job! Now what?

CHAPTER 6

What Do You Do About Leaving Home?

Bugging out can be a challenge for those not used to leaving home for long periods of time, particularly for anyone with pets, a spouse, and/or children. Long-distance relationships are never easy, and finding care for kids while either one or both parents are absent requires an extra support system. It can be a true test of the devotion of friends or family members when you ask for help with your adventure. Hopefully someone you trust can take care of your horse, dog, cat, goldfish, python, iguana, guinea pig, pet rat, spider collection, etc. Maybe your parents can look after a kid or two or help your spouse to manage daily life while you are away.

If you are single, where do you live? You might need a friend to house-sit for you. Or you may choose to sublet your home or apartment for a while to cover the rent/mortgage costs. Be sure to secure valuables or lock off one area for special stuff, put it in storage, or leave it with someone you trust. It's a good idea to have a friend or relative involved. Introduce them to the renter and let them know who they can contact should they need help for four to six months or more and both parties know who's who. But if leaving your place empty, just for safety's sake, as you may be posting on social media about your adventures, it's best if there is a neighbor or friend keeping some activity going on there to keep it protected. Get someone to mow the grass, set up lights on timers inside. If you have a security system, be sure someone else is listed for contact in case of activation; you will not be available! Some systems allow you to monitor the property on your cell phone no matter where you are, but there isn't much you can do from halfway around the world.

As for your car, if you have one, your options are: (1) park somewhere safe (preferably in a garage), disconnect the battery, and cover it up; (2) have someone you know well start it up and drive it around the block once a week or so; (3) loan it to someone you trust to use in your absence; or (4) you could make some extra cash by renting it out through a site like Turo. For the latter, you need someone local to manage the rental. Refer to the website for details at *https://Turo.com*. Check on how your insurance is set up to cover you, your vehicle, and the renter. If you choose to store it somewhere, check with your mechanic on the best treatment to protect engine, tires, and finish. Mine suggested a fuel treatment and an interior moisture absorber for leaving the car immobile for more than a month, especially in winter.

- ✓ Okay, home life — check
- ✓ Kid/pet care — check
- ✓ Vehicle care — check
- ✓ Valid passport in hand — check
- ✓ Medical completed — check
- ✓ Background check — check

Bills

Next, get your bills set up to pay online, and if you can arrange autopay, that's even better. Wi-Fi may not always be available, and knowing your bills are paid on time will provide financial peace of mind. Choose either balance payment in full or just the minimum due. Either way, you won't have to worry about lapsing credit card payments or your phone being turned off if you miss one. You most likely will be able to arrange a direct deposit of your paycheck to your bank so you will know when you will be paid and arrange when your bills tap the account so they will be covered to allow processing time and avoid overdrafts. There are money-transfer services available in most ports.

Banking

Try to arrange all banking for online access to check balances, transfer funds, etc. Give the bank a good emergency contact number among your family or close friends that they can call if necessary. If you need to add someone to your account so that they can manage transactions for you in an emergency, set that up.

Credit Cards

Confirm that your credit cards do not incur foreign transaction fees. Some banks have affiliates worldwide where you can obtain local currency with your debit card from the ATMs without fees. There is usually a list on the bank's website that pinpoints locations so you can see where the nearest ones are to your itinerary ports. Most European countries make traveling easy with the use of the Euro, and local currency can be easily obtained. Check online for the most current offers from major banks to choose the best one for you. There are many with no annual or foreign transaction fees. Confirm your potential destinations.

Cellphone

Be triple sure that the phone service you carry is appropriate to your destinations. Roaming is expensive, so find one that covers you wherever you will go. Once at sea, your phone may switch to Cellular at Sea, which is pricy. It's best to switch to airplane mode when sailing. The carrier T-Mobile works well for many with its international plans, but check into the current offers where you are enrolled to be sure there is adequate coverage to allow calls home or in the country, and enough data for your purposes. You may want to investigate a mobile hotspot.

Emergency Preparedness

Okay, this has to be said: regardless of your age and situation, it's a good idea to have a will prepared. (What!) Yes, ship life is generally a safe endeavor, but just like driving on freeways or flying in planes, literally anything can happen. Be sure your family has instructions should anything befall you either at sea or in another country. Astronauts always plan for a worst-case scenario to be completely prepared, and that is wise advice for anyone. Where would you like to (literally) end up? Your medical insurance is covered by the company, but God forbid, should there be a catastrophe of some sort, think ahead and consider what would happen if you didn't come back. They will send you home, but what do you want to happen to your stuff? Prepare a health directive should care be needed. Leave letters for your loved ones should you not get a chance to see them again. Having these details prepared for what you don't need is much better than needing them and not having them.

Leave a list of e-mail addresses and/or phone numbers of close friends that your family can notify, just in case. You can seal all this in an envelope and leave it with someone you trust or put it in a bank safe deposit box or personal safe to which someone else has access. This tough bit of forethought will let you head out into the world knowing that preparations have been made. It is *extremely* rare that this information will actually be needed, but it gives everyone peace of mind. In that safe place, leave such crucial information as your online passwords (or access to your master password for secure apps), your phone and computer access codes, bank account numbers, and PIN numbers, etc. Be sure to update the information periodically to keep it current (you know how often a new password is requested for your various accounts).

Story

I got suddenly very ill while I was in Mexico and was sent back to Miami for treatment. Since I'd been rolling solo for so long, I realized that while I was laid up without access to communication, nobody knew where my storage locker was, or where to find the key. No one knew which bank had my accounts and who would get my belongings once I no longer needed them. Plus, since I hadn't paid it, my phone bill lapsed, and my service was turned off. When I recovered, I had to completely reboot the phone and lost all my contacts and data! It was an eye-opener. Cloud backups are more important than ever! Once I was back home, I tried to minimize my extraneous stuff and write out some specifications of what should be done with my body and my belongings if perchance I didn't return. It's a good idea to discuss this with someone close to you as well, so should there be an emergency, the rest of the family, amid the emotional trauma of losing you, doesn't have to deal with decisions you have already contemplated. Just do it for everyone's peace of mind. A bit of preparation will make things easier on everyone. I was extremely well taken care of by the company. Obviously I went back to work, but it was a wake-up call to be prepared. I can carry on without worry.

Okay, enough about the hazards! Let's get back to the adventure side of it all!

Mail

Try to minimize as much snail mail as you can. Most anything that can be converted to paperless and Wi-Fi-accessible will keep things simpler: credit cards, phone bills, mortgage or rent payments, insurance renewals, etc. The autopay process will help. Of course, there will always be something that slips through and must be delivered. Be aware that once you have ordered something from a catalog, you will continue to receive not only that one but also others to whom your address may have been sold; check the phone number on the order form and request cancellation ASAP. It usually takes about three months for delivery to stop. Otherwise, they'll just pile up in your absence.

If you are on your own, in the United States there are mail services such as United Parcel Service (UPS), Postal Annex, or Federal Express (FedEx) locations. For a small fee, renewable by the month, by the quarter, or by the year, these services provide a mailbox with an actual street address rather than a post office box. You can call or e-mail them to see what may have been delivered in your absence. They can dispose of junk mail and/or forward mail to you for the cost of the postage (by weight) should you really need it. Or you can authorize a friend or family member to pick up for you.

Minimize as much mail as possible. It takes ages to receive any mail on the ship. If you must, you can obtain the mailing address for your ship from the Human Resources Department onboard. There is a central headquarters address for the company, and the mail is sorted by the ship name on the address label. It is then sent to the port agent at the embarkation port where the ship turns around the cruises. This could be anywhere in the world, from Singapore to Barcelona, Sydney to Seattle. Once the package is received at the port, it is then held until the ship arrives and is delivered to HR where it is sorted again by department. You should be notified by your department head that you have a package to retrieve from the office. This entire process could take months. If Mom really wants to send you cookies, they may be very stale by the time they arrive!

To help alleviate this complication, some ports in the world have facilities for crew that will help process mail for you if you visit them regularly, as long as your itinerary doesn't change. These kind folks, usually identified as "Seafarers Centers" will receive your mail/packages and keep them safe until you return to the center at the end of each cruise. Other crew members should be able to help you find this service at one of your home ports to secure the proper mailing address to use. Some locations work with the port agents to facilitate deliveries.

For online package orders, Amazon.com has set up collection boxes in various locations in the world for your purchases. There are over one thousand (nine hundred in the US) Amazon Hub Lockers worldwide, the locations of which can be located from their website by zip code, and there may be one nearby your port. When you order, you use that location as your shipping address. You receive an e-mail with a six-digit code when the item is delivered, and you have a designated number of days to pick it up. As long as the order will fit in the box, you're good to go. *But* check the delivery date carefully and place your order based on when you expect to arrive at that port to receive it, or the item will be sent back. These are lockers; a new keyboard will not fit! But if you're a musician and you've gotta have a new stomp box, a set of strings, reeds, or a cable, it's an option. You can also return items through the hub, but getting things off the ship can run into complications. It takes time to contact the security office days before you arrive to secure a landing form before you can take them out through security. This assures that you have receipts for purchases and proper packaging confirming that the items are indeed yours and don't belong to the ship! Order carefully!

Mail Story

A package was sent to me from San Diego when my ship was in Europe. It was forwarded from Miami to Civitavecchia, Italy. But it didn't arrive until after I had signed off the ship. I went home to San Diego without it. It took numerous phone calls to find out which shipping company had handled it and where it had gone. After about two months, I found that it had stayed onboard for a month before it was sent back to Miami. I checked with the mail room at headquarters repeatedly until I could locate its whereabouts. Once they confirmed that I was the recipient, I had to wait again to have it sent to my home and at my expense. I had to set up a FedEx account just to give the handler a way to charge it. Fortunately it was a fairly small package, so the cost was about $12, but still, it was a hassle and took absolutely forever! Good thing it wasn't cookies!

Wi-Fi

Try to imagine how you could live without Wi-Fi! Okay, take heart, there *is* Internet connection onboard, but your access is determined by the company policies and is limited by the time you have available from your work schedule, the devices you have with which to connect, and how much you want to pay. It may be excruciatingly slow. Sometimes there may be limited free access so you can complete online trainings, or the ship may be out of guest service status and allow more accessibility. There is a crew Internet café where there are computers provided, or you can tap in with your own device, but online access is often charged by the minute. The rate is less than what is paid by the guests, but nonetheless, the cost may be charged against your paycheck and can add up quickly if you tend to surf. There may be package deals available, but it's an expense for which you will want to budget. The least expensive option is to go ashore when time allows to find a restaurant (secure locations with Internet passwords are safer than open systems like Starbucks) where you can enjoy a coffee or a lunch (whoo-hoo, some food you haven't had onboard!). You can download movies or your plethora of e-mails to peruse later, at your leisure, onboard without the connection. Most department heads are allowed access to Wi-Fi, without charge, for business use, so if you have an urgent need, your supervisor will sometimes accommodate you for emergency access.

Travel Tools

1. *Passport*—Can't say it enough, this is the most important document you will need. When traveling or signing on, always keep it handy. Put a color photocopy of it somewhere else in your packing, such as a sealable bag for your important papers. If you don't already have a passport, *apply immediately!* Check online for your country's qualifications. In the United States, a passport application can be obtained online at *http://www.USA.gov*. You will need an official passport photo, which can be obtained either

at a post office or mailbox service such as UPS or FedEx. Processing can take up to several months, and if you don't have one and are called to travel on short notice, you will have to decline the offer as you cannot travel without a passport. Whenever you enter a country by air, you pass through a customs gate where an official will check you into the country with your passport and verify your identity, sometimes with fingerprints and additional photos taken. Your home nationality will determine into which countries you are allowed. If you have *any* criminal activity or legal proceedings on your record, you may be denied entry. If you are approved, your passport will be stamped allowing admission. US passports are valid for ten years—unless you do something criminal, and it is confiscated! When you get onboard your ship, it will be taken from you in exchange for your crew identification card and kept in the HR safe. There will be periodic immigration checks for which it will be returned to you just long enough to queue up and show to an official, then it goes back into the vault until you disembark.

2. *Passport card*—In the US there is an option to add a passport card for an additional charge. This card can be backup to your regular passport. It is not a substitute, but it's convenient when entering ports in the US, and it fits more easily in your wallet. Should you misplace your regular passport, the card would facilitate a replacement. It also serves as an alternative identification card while your booklet-type passport is being held onboard, especially handy if you (heaven forbid) miss the ship!

3. *TSA/Global Entry*—In addition to your passport, in the United States, you can obtain a frequent traveler identity number through the United States Office of Homeland Security. There is a charge, but if you travel often, it pays for itself quickly. You can find a location online and must arrange a personal appointment. An agent will ask a few questions, check your passport and/or driver's license, take

your fingerprints, and enter your photo and information into an international database. *TSA* enrollment allows you access to a quicker airport security line where you are not required to take off shoes, belts, light jackets, nor remove electronics from your carry-on. Your enrollment can be remotely renewed after five years. *Global Entry* is an additional qualification card that facilitates entry back into the United States from foreign countries. Instead of waiting in excessively long security lines, Global Entry allows you to bypass that huge line, slip your passport into a kiosk, get a clearance receipt, and allows you through the customs gate as a preapproved traveler. Well worth the interview time and extra expense. Getting both together is the most cost-effective plan.

4. *ClearMe*—In addition to the TSA PreCheck, in the US, there is an additional service that makes American airport entry even easier. Based in New York City, ClearMe provides their own lanes to security in sixty-five airports in the United States (at this time), and it is always expanding to more locations and other countries. For updated information, go to *www.ClearMe.com*. In a separate shorter security lane, an actual person escorts you through the kiosk process to validate your identity through fingerprints or retinal scan. You will be taken directly to the security agent who will allow you to cut the line and go straight to the electronic scanning. The cost is $179 per year USD, but if you are signed up for the Delta Airlines mileage program, the cost is reduced to $119 per year. Again this service can save you tremendous amounts of time and make your airport experience much easier. If you also have TSA PreCheck, you go to that line for even quicker entry to the boarding areas. If you are running late for a flight, this service will save the day!

Travel Story

I signed up for ClearMe online but had not activated the service in person. I live on an island and have to rely on the ferry schedule to get to the mainland airport. I misread the Sunday ferry schedule and was counting on a 7:30 a.m. boat to make it to the airport. I took a taxi to the ferry dock only to find no boat! *What?* I had to wait an hour for the next one. I anxiously caught a taxi to the airport and hustled through baggage check. Arriving at security, the line was super long, but the ClearMe kiosk was right there with a smiling lady who said, "Are you a ClearMe member?"

"Yes," I replied, "but I never finished the application."

"No problem," she said calmly. "You will make it, come with me." She took a quick photo of my anxious face in the machine, put my fingers on the keypad, and voila! My name appeared, she marked my boarding pass and walked me past this immense line to the very front, showed my boarding pass to the TSA security agent, and I went right to the x-ray belt for carry-ons. Since I had TSA PreCheck on my boarding pass, everything went through without removing anything. Rushing off to my gate, I arrived just as they were starting to board. Whew! Thank you, ClearMe!

Advice

Remember to take a photo of your luggage just in case it is misplaced by the airline. Take note of the brand. It's easier to show a picture and give them a description and the manufacturer name of the luggage to help them track it down. It will usually be delivered to your hotel or to the ship if necessary. Keep this photo in your favorites for easy access.

CHAPTER 7

Packing and Traveling

Luggage

Perhaps you have been putting off the inevitable—borrowing from family or friends or getting by with Grandad's old American Tourister. In college, some guys tossed everything into big black garbage bags! Well, you can't check a garbage bag on an airplane, so it may be time to dive into the market and get the perfect bag for *you*. Shop around, talk to others, ask questions, remember the ship-storage situation, and compare quality and prices. A broken wheel can be the worst! I've found that a twenty-four-inch rolling bag is as big as I can go without incurring overweight charges. Bigger than that is far too easy to overfill and harder to "drive."

Your carry-on can be a roller board (limited to about 21"×15"×10") that will fit in the overhead compartment, and/or a rolling backpack, or a soft strap-to-the handle tote that can fit under the seat in front of you. As mentioned in the ship cabin layout section, be aware that there is no extra space for luggage storage, so your best bet is under the bed. A rolling duffel or a top loader won't take up much room when unpacking, unlike a clam-shell bag. Take the prospective bag for a walk around the store; imagine how you would arrange your belongings and what it will feel like full. For organizing the inside, you may want to opt for the compact travel bags to segregate your things, or use the compressible plastic space-saver bags (just be sure to get the travel ones that will roll the air out, not the ones requiring a vacuum cleaner). Be absolutely positive that it is (a) *very* durable and waterproof; (b) has decent-sized strong zippers with substantial zipper pulls; (c) an easily accessible, strong, telescoping handle; and (d) a way to lock it efficiently. You may want to add a luggage strap around it for extra security, but beware, that little extra might disappear if TSA decides to scrutinize the bag as it may not always make its way back onto your bag; fortunately, these are inexpensive. The beds onboard are often a max of about 15 inches off the floor, and some are only 11.5 inches high. There is only about 2.5 feet of space across the middle of the room, so a clam-shell style hard case won't lay flat unless you drag it up onto the bottom bunk. And try to avoid black bags! There are *way* too many out there, and yours could be easily mistaken for someone else's. Pack things tightly to minimize any potential damage.

Be sure your bag has adequate identification. Some bags have their own little ID pocket for your contact information where it is not readily visible. I like having a colorful luggage tag in addition. List just your name, phone, and/or e-mail address. It's also a good idea to put a sheet of paper inside your bag on top of your packing with your contact information as well. If the outside bag tags are lost, you can be located. And as they often announce at baggage carousels, "many bags look alike." Create personalized identification for yours with things like a yarn pom-pom, a fabric ribbon, or a bright-colored bandana.

Once you have your luggage, give yourself plenty of time in advance of departure to assemble what you *think* you want to take. Lay it all out and reassess what goes with what. If I loaded the bag now, would it all fit? Hmm, maybe skip the extra jeans or the onesie. Leave yourself time to reassess, take out, replace, or reconsider. Remember your potential activities and weather potentials. Packing in advance gives you a chance to sleep on your decisions and make a list of things you may think of later. Consider the extreme case that your luggage should become lost in transit—don't take things that are irreplaceable. Distribute the weight evenly and put anything heavy on the end where the wheels are. Put shoes, sole out, along the edges or put them in bags to keep clothing clean. Consider the length and locations of your contract. I started one in the summer heat of the Caribbean and ended in a cold November in the northeast of the US and had to do a shopping run for a warm coat!

Packing

So now you're ready. You have received a reservation for a plane ticket to somewhere, and a LOE (a letter of employment) that confirms that you are indeed employed. How do you pack for four, six, nine months or more? If your position involves a required uniform (usually available onboard), your packing will be primarily for your off-duty wear for port travel and crew bar casual/party wear. Depending on your position, you may be required to have formal wear. And remember, the cabins are small, so don't overdo the packing! Today you can go to *www.YouTube.com* and search for "cruise crew cabins" to see videos of their accommodations. Frankly just about anything you leave behind you can replace in most of the ports of call and will be contributions to your souvenir collection. Pack once, then take out half!

Always remember to put your passport somewhere secure but easily accessible as you travel; you will need it often.

Consider these elements in packing:

1. Stay within the weight restrictions of the airline. Typically maximum fifty pounds or twenty-seven kilos. Usually the company will cover the cost of one bag, but check. Anything more will be carry-on or at personal expense. Weigh on a flat bathroom scale at home, then double-check before handing them off to airport agents.
2. Luggage needs to be light and best to fit under the bed somehow (possibly between eleven and fifteen inches high); no extra storage space.
3. You have to be able to carry everything in one trip (and do it several times)—by yourself!

4. Mixy-matchy clothing is more versatile than onesies, and try to avoid anything that needs dry cleaning or ironing!
5. Layers are ideal. Check the temperatures for outside (Celsius? What is that in Fahrenheit, please?). The ship will be air-conditioned, but is that outdoor heat going to be dry or humid? *Try everything on!* Assemble all the bits that go with it: shoes, jewelry, accessories, etc. You will live with this for months, so be sure it fits well, is in good condition, comfortable, and attractive on your shape. Laundry onboard can involve hard water, so don't take anything irreplaceable. If your job is actually *in* the laundry, it's gonna be hot, and you will be issued uniform clothing that is appropriate!
6. If you are not in uniform, formal nights mean tuxes or dark suits for the gentlemen and gowns for the ladies. Nothing too revealing, extra tight, super short, or low cut, please.
7. Shoe choices can be a challenge. In uniform, the guidelines will be provided on what to buy. Otherwise I have seen girls onboard trying to totter down the metal crew hallways in their big platforms to stage or crew bar, and as awesome as they look, they are (a) very painful for long hours, and (b) really dangerous on a moving ship when you must keep your balance. If you absolutely insist, take flats to get you where you're going and back. And you really don't want to end up in medical and out of work with a sprained ankle! Yes, I've seen it happen! Men, just a plain pair of black, preferably tie-on shoes will do.
8. Laundry. There is a crew laundry available for your use with numerous washers and dryers. You could use one of your luggage bags for laundry collection and transporting to the laundry area. An invaluable item is a lingerie bag for underwear and socks that keeps you from losing things in the machines; please save the orphan socks from the dryer trolls; this way they stay together. The dryers are stacked on top of the washers, and although there is usually a step stool available, it's easy to overlook small bits in the big

dryer. Stay close or set an alarm to return to assure that you are out of the machines on time. Don't let things disappear by not being responsible for your stuff. Others are waiting.
9. Detergent can be purchased from either the slop chest or in port. Flakes, pods, or sheets are easier to manage than bottled liquids. Water can be "hard," so dryer sheets are helpful to soften and minimize static, again available in most ports. Don't even think about bringing a clothing iron. Items with heating coils will be confiscated; there are built-in ironing facilities in the crew laundry and are supplied for uniform maintenance.

So what to pack for personal stuff? As a performer, I had a handle on stage wardrobe options, but I had no idea what to wear in Australia! Back in college, I traveled with a group to China to see the Great Wall. The pictures from that trip horrify me to this day. I had no clue! I was dressed in jeans and a blue cotton shirt with a giant penguin on it, and I wore wedgie platform shoes (hey, they were cute and went with the outfit!). Bear in mind, this is a surface made of ancient uneven and weathered stones, all laid on steep inclines! Needless to say, dumb-da-dumb-dumb! I had to hold onto someone most of the time to stand up and looked like an ignorant tourist in my completely inappropriate outfit! I missed a lot of the experience watching the ground for fear of falling flat on my face. I learned that it was imperative to do some research on the culture's customs, the weather expectations, and the potential activities. Blend in, be practical, and don't be stupid.

My first ship contract was a repositioning run from Alaska to Australia. I joined the ship in Honolulu, stopping in Tahiti, Moorea, Bora Bora, and New Zealand before arriving in Sydney. Heading for Down Under, I realized it was going to be very hot and humid. I found out the hard way that the southern sun was exceptionally brutal, and I managed to get my very pale self well fried more than once. Light denim jeans are okay (*no* holey knees allowed, by the way). Skip the swimsuit cover up and buy big T-shirts from the local tourist shops as souvenirs. Comfortable walking shoes are essential, and don't forget a hat and sunscreen! Ship contracts usually follow the summer, wherever that is.

My second contract took me to Europe, and again, don't look like a clueless tourist for several important reasons. If you wear wild clothes, excessive jewelry, flashing an expensive camera, you are literally broadcasting, "Please rob me!" Perceptions around the world of tourists are often misconceptions of excessive wealth. Not to be paranoid, but it is just basic common sense; you don't want to be a target. If you have the money for designer clothes and bags, others may "request the donation" of everything you've got—which may include threats to your life. If you've got the goodies, leave them at home; they'll be there to enjoy when you get back. Stay low-key wherever possible. The fashionable fuchsia hair color may be fun back home (and not be uniform approved), but standing out in a strange country may attract more attention than you bargained for. Just sayin'.

Other stuff that I found helpful to have include the following:

1. *Luggage*—A rolling duffel will collapse and fit under the bed. Opt for sturdy luggage construction with really good wheels. If you need more space to get stuff home, you will find options in port to augment your luggage collection if necessary.
2. *A large closed water bottle*—Many ships have a bottle filler in the crew areas like the ones in airports. This saves lots of plastic and keeps you hydrated, as ship air is very drying. Bottled water is also available for purchase from the slop chest, and the plastic is dutifully recycled.
3. *A laptop*—Some sort of computer is helpful for movies and journaling. I also carry a large multiterabyte external hard drive for movies and a couple of little flash drives to be able to exchange smaller files with others who are often willing to share some of their movie collections or workout routines.
4. *Hair-dryer/curling iron/hot rollers*—For any of these, check that yours doesn't draw too much power. I blew a circuit on an older Norwegian ship with my hair dryer, which did

not go over well with the facilities team. Consider a multiconfiguration power converter. On rare occasions, you may find yourself in a hotel for which you need an adapter, depending on your country of origin; check your itinerary.

5. *Three-way multiplug adapter*—Most ships have European round-pronged plugs and a couple of American spaded-plug outlets in the cabins. As there are so few, to share a cabin with others requires some creative plugging. Security will confiscate power strips unless they have been approved, but a simple three-way plug that accommodates two-prong cords won't overload an outlet. A multi-USB port or multi-hub is also helpful for phones, cameras, earbuds, and other similar accessories.

6. *An extension cord*—Okay, this is kind of "if-y" on the acceptable list, but if it's a basic two-pronged, non-grounded cord, it may we wimpy enough to be acceptable. Your outlet is most often on the opposite side of the room from the bed. If you like to charge your phone and keep it handy, or use your laptop, the only way to manage that is to use a six to ten-foot phone cable and at least a six to eight-foot extension cord, which also provides extra outlets.

7. *Bathroom accessories and/or makeup*—Be aware that not all your favorite makeup or bath brands may be available worldwide. If you're happy with more generic brands, they are usually obtainable in ports. A suction-cup mounted makeup mirror might be helpful. Bathroom lighting is better than in the cabin, and there is no counter space.

8. *Medications*—Bring enough for a month at least, along with your prescriptions. The onboard medical facility can assist in replenishment. If you ever find yourself afflicted with a serious malady, the medical staff will transfer you to a hospital on the immediate itinerary. If you are incapacitated in some way, your department head will be responsible for packing your belongings from your cabin and send them to a port agent for safekeeping until you are released, either to return to the ship (once you are cleared) or sent home. The

medical facility is truly the power center regarding your continued stay onboard, and they reserve the right to recommend disembarkation to the captain should they deem it in the best interest of either you or the others onboard the ship. Bring what you need to stay healthy, but know you will be well cared for.

9. *Wallets*—If you are headed for countries that use foreign currency, it's helpful to keep all that coinage separated. You may encounter several countries in your contract that may include the US, Canada, the UK, Mexico, Euro countries, non-Euro countries, New Zealand, Australia, etc.
10. *Waterproof camera*—Whether using your phone or a "real" camera, if you want to capture the amazing fish below the waves or your friends on a sandy beach, it is wise to take either a waterproof case or a dedicated waterproof camera to capture those special experiences. For fear of damaging my device, I missed many amazing shots of swimming with stingrays in Bora Bora!

Personal stuff—Some things like laundry soap, shower gel or soap, mouthwash, lotion, or shampoo are available in the slop chest, local markets, or Seafarers' Centers worldwide. For some of these, bring just enough to get you through the first few weeks until you find your port sources. But at home, you don't have to worry about foreign currency or the availability of the brands you like, and using things up creates space/weight available for things you will buy to take home. Choose carefully.

Girl stuff/makeup:
a. Powder
b. Foundation
c. Eyeliner
d. Mascara
e. Lipstick

Guy stuff:
a. Shaving cream
b. Razors/blades (or electric)
c. Body lotion
d. Hair gel/mousse
e. Deodorant

WORK AT SEA, SEE THE WORLD: AN INSIDER'S SECRETS TO THE WORKING LIFE ON A CRUISE SHIP

f. Makeup remover
g. Sunblock
h. Body lotion
i. Facial moisturizer
j. Nail polish/travel size (or pads) remover
k. Hair gel/mousse
l. Shampoo/conditioner
m. Deodorant (your favorite brand)
n. Toothbrush (electric is fine, with charger; a charge may last weeks)
o. Toothpaste
p. Dental floss
q. Loofa, mitt, or washcloth (face cloth may not always be issued onboard)
r. Tampons, pads, liners, etc. (your usual brands may not be available)
s. Fragrance (there are crew sales onboard)
t. Blow-dryer/curling iron/rollers
u. Brush/comb

f. Toothbrush (electric okay)
g. Toothpaste
h. Dental floss
i. Fragrance (onboard sales)
j. Sunblock (slop chest)
k. Blow-dryer if you need it/comb

Damn, it's so much easier to be a guy!

Packing Hacks to Consider

Stuff your socks into your shoes. Be sure anything liquid is in a securely sealed container, and double bag if necessary. Simplify the cosmetics (one cream, not three). Use a plastic-lined bag or a ziplock. Tuck in a few Band-Aids. A small roll of packing tape for mailing things home. A little something that feels like home (a lavender sachet, your favorite herbal tea, a family photo). Button and zip everything before folding, rolling, or bagging. Slipping plastic dry-cleaner bags between layers will help minimize wrinkles without adding weight. If you opt for the duffel, the best system is either rolling everything, using compression bags, or the plastic space bags to keep things in order. The joy of this trip is that other than travel and next-day clothes, you will be able to completely unpack once onboard. Top it off with your ID page in a plastic sleeve to make it usable for the return trip.

Pack your carry-on with the more important elements such as meds, medical forms, travel munchies, jewelry (keep that minimal and inexpensive), and electronics. *Be sure* to keep your passport somewhere safe but accessible, like a zippered pocket or purse. You will need medical forms on arrival at the port, so have them handy in carry-on bags for easy locating.

Things I Have Found Useful to Take

I know I said keep it light, but these were some miscellaneous things you might find useful.

1. *Something for your cards*—A retractable pocket lanyard (available onboard from HR) will clip your essential access cards together. Most cards are hole-punched for this. However, some newer ships have magnetically read key cards that cannot be punched. For this, a plastic sleeve or multipocket credit card case will help keep them together. Protect your cards from your phone, earbuds, or anything with a magnetic clasp as they can demagnetize them easily.

Don't get stranded in the hall, having to track down security late at night, or having to wait to get cards remagnetized when HR opens. Cards you will need to carry at all times will be:
- Crew photo ID card—also used for any purchases onboard, leaving or boarding the ship in ports; has your photo, crew number, and date of expiration. You trade in your passport for this and relinquish it when you finish your contract and sign off.
- Cabin door key card—usually it's blank, so remember your cabin number.
- Emergency card—this details your emergency number, drill location and other emergency duties. It may be green, red, white, or blue. The color and markings will define which drills in which you are required to participate.

2. *Medium-sized light daypack/backpack or tote bag*—For port adventures, be prepared to carry whatever you need: laptop, phone, charging cables, sweatshirt, beach towel, umbrella, water bottle, camera, etc.
3. *Headphones and/or earbuds*—Handy for gym or computer work, or getting to sleep; don't disturb your roomie and be able to watch or listen to whatever *you* like; noise cancelling for airplane use are great. Not allowed to be used in traffic areas.
4. *Earplugs*—If you like some quiet, these are important; others may snore. Having these handy can help maintain some harmony with roommates. You may also find that your cabin is located near a noisy area like a high traffic hallway, the crew mess, gym, bar, disco, or just loud neighbors. Good for airplanes too. If you wonder if it's you that snores, the app SnoreLab will record you at night and help determine if you should address apnea issues, want to invest in nose strips, or a dental appliance to minimize the issue.

5. *Sleep mask*—In the same vein, if you like it dark, and your roommate has other ideas, this helps a lot. It allows both you and your roommate a bit of privacy if you're working on different schedules, and also invaluable for long airplane flights. If you are fortunate to have a cabin window/porthole, sometimes the sunrise occurs earlier than you were planning to wake up. A few clothespins or chip clips for securing curtains that don't quite close sufficiently will help too.
6. *Cell phone*—You already know how indispensable it is! With the ship's digital apps these days, often you need to virtually sign onboard or attend online trainings. WhatsApp can be useful, and with some carriers, you can phone home from selected ports.
7. *Small analogue battery-powered alarm clock*—Often you may have multiple time changes announced as you trot around the globe. Your cell phone may update on its own—or not! Beware. Having a clock that doesn't take up one of the precious plugs and can be adjusted manually will help you know what time it *really* is. It is easily adjusted forward or back according to the ship directions, and you don't want to miss a training, or even worse, a work schedule because you were in the wrong time zone or your phone didn't update! It's also easy to see in the cabin and keep nearby.
8. *Camera*—The best you can afford but small enough to be convenient. Save the memories. A cell phone camera is often adequate, but you may want a waterproof camera if you plan to do water sports or a real camera if you are into serious photography. A selfie stick or portable tripod can be helpful for creative shots, expanding the range, or chronicling your adventures when there is nobody around that you would trust with your device to help you out. You may visit places you will only see once, so keep those memories alive with photos. A valuable tip I received was to grab a shot of the info sign on the gangway before leaving the ship

as you disembark to remember the date, where you were, and what time you are due back onboard.

9. *Sewing kit*—If you know how to sew, bring a compact kit of basic colors of thread, needles, small tape measure, and little scissors. There is usually a tailor onboard, but he/she is always busy and keeps strange hours. It is best if you can fix things yourself or find a crew member who can help. If you're in a pickle, track down the theater cast member who is in charge of the costumes, and they can usually help you out. Be sure to overpay them for their services, be it in cash, a bottle of their favorite drink, or a bag of snacks.

10. *Mesh lingerie bag*—For everybody, keep your socks together in the laundry! No sense in creating orphans or fattening the dryer trolls; singles have a magical way of getting stuck in the dryer.

11. *Magnetized clips*—Cabin walls are metal and make it easy to hang photos, maps, etc. for a touch of home.

12. *Stick-on/removable closet hooks*—Command-brand hooks are handy to put inside the closet door and removable at the end, or be nice and leave them for the next guy. Extra hanging space!

13. *Collapsible umbrella*—Sturdy enough to withstand some wind but small enough to pack easily; shade in intense heat or shelter from the rain. It will happen, more often than you expect, and can blow in from anywhere without warning at any time!

14. *Rainwear*—A light foldable rain jacket or plastic poncho.

15. *Sun hat, baseball cap, and/or sun visor*—Sun intensity is not the same worldwide. In some parts of the world, it is really powerful, and you don't want to get fried. Flat and packable and wide-brimmed is best, with a chin strap as it was often very windy, especially on the docks.

16. *Manicure set*—Clippers and nail files to smooth out rough spots.

17. *Chargers/cables*—For whatever needs them: camera, phone, iPad/tablet, computer, recorder, etc. I've found a small five-

port multi-USB charger port be helpful for charging pad, phone, earbuds, etc. at once and using only one power outlet. A six or ten-foot phone cord can be helpful.

18. *Flip-flops and/or reef shoes*—Many beaches in the world are rocky, have strange critters on the bottom, or sand that can be very hot. I wish I had had them in Thailand when I went to swim with the elephants in a rocky stream—ouch!
19. *Slip-on shoes*—Quite often port entry/exit for crew requires x-ray screening, including shoes. Slip-off/on keeps the line moving.
20. *Swimsuit*—European ladies wear bikinis no matter what shape they are in (and they make them in *all* sizes!). Wear whatever is comfortable for you, but be prepared to enjoy beaches nearly everywhere.
21. *Magnifying makeup mirror*—For me, a lifesaver! I like a seven-inch 5× magnification; suction-cup mounted (moisten the suction cups before attaching to the mirror). Bathroom medicine cabinets are often very high. If you're vertically challenged, this will help a lot.
22. *Padlock(s)*—Drawers and/or closets can be secured for your valuables, and sometimes a safe is provided. You can use your TSA luggage locks.
23. *Batteries*—A few extra for whatever runs on them (clock, camera, etc.); AAs, AAA, etc.
24. *Snorkel, mask, and fins*—If you are planning a lot of swimming and snorkeling. These items are usually rentable at the locations, but if you have your own and can afford the space and weight, at least you know they fit, and yours is the only mouth that's been involved in the use thereof. Here's to hoping you get some time off and enjoy them!
25. *Binoculars*—Handy for scouting the ports, watching for whales, finding birds in tropical forests, identifying passing ships, watching for strange things in the ocean or on the shoreline.

Items Not Allowed

Seems obvious, but just in case:

1. *Iron*—Anything with a heating element is a fire hazard. Your luggage is x-rayed upon boarding, and these items will be confiscated. There are irons in the crew laundry room.
2. *Weapons*—Knives, guns, fireworks, other such falderal. *Never* try to take these onboard! *Ever.*
3. *Candles*—Sorry to deflate the romantic inclinations, but *never* should you have an open flame onboard. No candles or incense. If you just can't live without them, get the battery-operated ones. Also useful as a bathroom night-light.
4. *Lighters*—Much like an airport, butane lighters are not allowed; the disposables or just paper matches are passable these days for those who smoke. They are usually available in the slop chest.
5. *Power strips*—Security is strict about too much plugging in. Stick to nongrounded cords.
6. *Restraints*—You may have some explaining to do when security finds the fuzzy pink handcuffs. Sorry, too bad. Confiscated.

Double checklist:

☐	Passport	In hand
☐	Home/apartment	Someone to look after it: rent, sublet, house-sitter
☐	Kids/pets	Ditto
☐	Car	Ditto here too
☐	Bills	Online or autopay
☐	Rent/mortgage	Autopay
☐	Phone	Correct SIM card or cell plan
☐	Credit card(s)	No foreign exchange fees

☐	Utilities	Autopay
☐	Insurance	Ditto
☐	Emergency list	Compilation of pertinent information
☐	Health directive	Completed and signed
☐	Will	Completed and signed with witnesses
☐	Mail	Collection and management arranged
☐	Travel enrollments?	Depending on how often you travel and what country you are in:

- ○ Airline milage membership (those miles add up)
- ○ TSA
- ○ Global Entry
- ○ ClearMe

Okay, I'm guessing you have traveled before. But if not, here's some advice. As mentioned above, most airlines limit the weight of such to a maximum of fifty US pounds or twenty-seven kilos, but check the limitations from your particular airline and your ship requirements. It is advisable to weigh your bag on a home bathroom scale to assure that you are within the limits. *Before* arriving at check-in at the airport, find an open scale and confirm the weight again for accuracy to be sure you don't need to rearrange to meet the weight limit. Anything over, you have to carry onboard yourself or pay fees. I usually pack a few removable bits on top just in case. Be sure that you have packed anything that may be in violation of TSA regulation in your larger checked bag and secure it with a TSA-approved lock. This includes any liquid or gel in a container larger than three ounces, any sort of powdered substance (such as dietary protein supplement), or any sort of liquid (shampoo). In a carry-on, I've learned that protein powder looks like explosives, and a harmonica is easily mistaken for a gun clip! If you are borrowing your girlfriend's laptop, and you are asked to turn it on, never say, "Oh, this isn't mine!"

WORK AT SEA, SEE THE WORLD: AN INSIDER'S SECRETS TO THE WORKING LIFE ON A CRUISE SHIP

You are allowed only two carry-on items. To minimize boarding time at the gate, airlines encourage you to check roller-board bags, a wheeled bag that fits in the overhead compartment, and limited to about twenty-one inches by fifteen inches by ten inches. If your economy ticket requires boarding farther down the line, you may find that space is maxed out, and they will insist that you check the bag anyway at no charge. It is advisable to have a TSA-approved lock ready for that one too. Keep anything with a lithium battery with you, along with medications, or anything you really need in-flight. An extra shirt, your pajamas, and essential overnight stuff would be wise to pack in carry-on just in case checked bags are mislaid or don't make an airline connection.

Your personal item is best as a soft bag or backpack that will fit under the seat in front of you, or even in the overhead if it is squishable. I like a rolling backpack. I can wear it until other bags are checked, then roll it. It protects my electronics, and once my other carry-on is checked in at the gate, I can take the weight off and roll it though large airports to make a connection, and it fits beneath the seat during the flight. Beware, however, that aisle seats are often narrower than middle seats, and windows seats may have a curve from the fuselage which may force you to put your bag in the overhead anyway. Planes are all different. Keep essential items (headphones, devices, books, etc.) easily accessible. Keep all your important papers with you (medical forms, LOE, etc.) in case of delays. If you have both a tote bag and a purse or briefcase, once the carry-on is gate-checked, you still have the maximum allotted of two items to carry onto the plane. Once you arrive, remember, you've got to carry everything you have—one trip—by yourself. If *anything* does not arrive on the baggage carousel, notify the airline *immediately*, and they will track it down and deliver either to your hotel or the ship before it sails. One reason you're sent there the night before. Take a photo of your bags and put it in your "favorites" photo file in your phone.

Baggage Story

Flying to Rome, Italy, I was routed through Amsterdam. The flight was delayed, I missed my connection, but my bags were already checked through to Rome. I managed to contact the crew travel center that got me on a flight on another airline so I could get to the ship on time, but the bags were sent later. On arrival, I had missed the crew bus but saw that the guest transport was still collecting passengers for the drive to the port. I reported my missing bags (with pictures!) and hitched a ride with the guests. I made it to the ship but had nothing with me but my electronics and pj's. The ship graciously provided a toiletry bag and a company T-shirt. I soon realized how little I really needed to survive for several days. We left Rome and sailed to the Greek islands where I had an excuse to buy a T-shirt and a sun hat. The bags finally arrived when we arrived in Athens several days later, carefully zip-tied from security check. Whew!

Important: As you may spend a night in a hotel prior to boarding the ship, put all you need for one overnight (pajamas, makeup, toiletries, medications, underwear, tomorrow's clothes, phone chargers, etc.) into the backpack or tote bag. In that case, you can leave your one or two big bags with the hotel bell captain or front desk. This minimizes the need to drag multiple heavy bags into elevators or down long carpeted hallways. (Remember to tip the bellman for the assistance.)

Checklist:

- Travel info—flights, hotel, contact information for your hiring agent/travel agent
- Medical forms
- Passport
- Cell phone/foreign SIM card if necessary
- Laptop
- Charging cables for everything
- Plane amusement materials
- Overnight supplies

- Checkable luggage
- Carry-on luggage
- Cash in small bills (for shuttle, baggage-handler tips, etc.). See info on destination currency later.

Airline Preparedness

The cruise line will send transportation information for your arrival at the destination airport. Unless the ship departs from a location near your home, your flight will be scheduled for arrival the day before your first cruise begins and will include a reservation for a hotel room. This allows for time zone differences, airline delays, lost bags, etc. Once you have the confirmation code, check the airline's website to make any seating changes you would like such as window, aisle, or location. Any upgrades will be at your expense as your ticket will be economy class. As for meals, the fare is pretty limited. Some people choose to bring veggie snacks or pick up munchies at the airport. For long flights, the airline website may detail the meal options, if any. You can sometimes order a special meal that meets your dietary requirements such as low cholesterol, kosher, or vegetarian. If you request a special meal, to ensure you get it, do this:

1. Order your selection online.
2. Call the airline the day before the flight to reiterate your order. Get the name of the person to whom you spoke, as well as the record locator number.
3. When you check in to the flight, ask if your meal is listed in the computer.
4. Prepare a note with the type of meal, your name, and your seat number and give it to the galley attendant as you board and ask if it has been loaded.

Entertainment

Many airlines these days only provide onboard digital entertainment (movies, TV shows, music) to be accessed from your personal device. Download the airline's app before you go. Be sure your devices are charged, and take the power cords. Remember a good set of headphones (noise-cancelling are preferable). For phones or tablets, a case or foldable stand is immensely helpful.

Twenty-four hours before departure, check in with your airline online. Check again for your meal. Get yourself to the airport with lots of time to spare for unhurried baggage check, security screening, and gate location. More travel details later. Enjoy your flight; take advantage of the Wi-Fi (it will be a while before you will have time and/or access on the ship) and the in-flight entertainment. The time will literally fly by. Napping is best with a good travel pillow, sleep mask, and earplugs or headphones. Sit back, relax, and enjoy the ride! You're on your way to adventure!

All my bags are packed, I'm ready to go…

—John Denver

CHAPTER 8

How Do You Sign On?

More about flying

You are on your way at last. Hopefully you have a short flight, but you may be crossing some time zones. If you are unaccustomed to the concept of potential jet lag, here is a bit of travel advice from an airline attendant that may be of help. There is the *physical* adjustment to hurry up and wait to get to the flight, followed by the inactivity of being sedentary for hours on end. There are the *emotional* issues of baggage stowing, "someone's in my seat," or deciding who gets the common armrest. Then there is the *spiritual* jetlag experience for those who may be concerned about the very concept of sitting in a metal tube shooting through the air at 555 miles per hour at thirty thousand feet above the ground. Here are a few techniques to help minimize the effects.

Reacclimation to new time zones can be a challenge, but generally east-to-west time changes are much easier on the body and mind than the reverse. Some ways to mitigate the changes include the following:

1. When you first buckle up, set your watch (or phone) to the local time at your arrival destination. This will help your mental clock start to adjust your biological cycles.

2. Adjust your in-flight sleep cycle to coincide with your arrival time. If you are to arrive in the morning, try to sleep as much as you can. If it's an evening arrival, either nap lightly or try to hold out to sleep after arrival. When you hit the hotel, you will drop off easily.
3. En route, envision your emotional scenario to "see" yourself arriving safe, alert, healthy, and happy, and anticipate the joys of your new adventure.

It is advisable to take your own food, even if the flight is long enough to serve you a meal. Airline food seems typically high in fat, sugar, and salt. Then when you are thirsty, the soft drinks are just as bad, so instead, drink plenty of water. If you ordered a special meal, confirm that it is onboard. Have your own choice of snacks and skip the salty pretzels.

Enjoy the entertainment options. Whether on the seat-mounted system or the app available for your device, take advantage of the opportunity to see some flicks you haven't seen, listen to an audiobook, or groove to your favorite music. Or you could read a book (a what!).

To keep yourself "moving," try some "seat yoga." Slowly contract and release every muscle you can think of from the bottom up: feet, legs, pelvis, chest, arms, neck, face. March in your seat by alternating bringing your knees up, rotate wrists and ankles. If you can, every couple of hours, when it's clear to do so, get up and walk. Go to the open space near the restroom and do some deep knee bends or squat for a minute or two and rock forward and back a little. If they are idle, chat up the attendants who, if not busy, are often happy to talk to you, offer you more water or extra snacks.

Getting some sleep. This is the advice of flight attendant Diana Fairechild in her book *Jet Smart*. To help you sleep, try this process. Carry-on prep: (1) a small bottle of drinking water; (2) an eye mask, preferably with the words "Do Not Disturb" on it (or taped on); (3) earplugs; (4) inflatable or beanbag neck pillow; (5) snacks; (6) essential oil; (7) large cotton hanky; and (8) toiletry kit of travel toothbrush/paste and facial moisturizer. When seated, dab a little oil into your nostrils. Once in the air, recline your seat. Swaddle yourself with sweater and blanket into a cocoon, but buckle your seat belt on the outside so the attendant won't wake you should there be a need. Wet the hanky with the water and cover your nose and mouth for a personal humidifier. Put the neck pillow in place and slip in your earplugs (or headphones) and lastly your sleep mask. Take deep breaths and relax. Imagine something peaceful to calm your mind. Imagine you are in your happy place.

For extra long flights, a holistic assistance remedy, usually available at travel stores, called *No-Jet-Lag* works well. It is an herbal tablet formulated to be consumed once at takeoff, and again every few hours (if you are awake). A seventeen-hour flight to Australia could have you arriving fresh as a daisy, much to the amazement of everyone else.

For a step further, if the plane is large, and the flight is not full, in your walkabout, take note of any empty aisles. Attendants will certainly allow you to move if you like, and you can pull up the armrests and at least get partially horizontal if you like. Grab an airline pillow and a blanket, seat belt outside, pop in the earplugs, and don your sleep mask for a nice rest. Before landing, stop by the restroom to brush teeth, comb hair, splash a little water on your face, and remoisturize. You'll arrive rested and ready to go.

Arrival

Welcome to wherever in the world! Did you have a nice flight? See some good movies? Get a nap? The ship is expecting you. Upon arrival at the airport in the port city, you will most likely be picked up by a ship agent at the baggage area and transported with other crew members to a hotel. Watch for signage for your company. If not, you will get instructions on where to go in your travel directive. If you need to take a taxi, most will accept credit cards. Have a basic overnight supply of clothing and bath stuff easily available, preferably in your carry-on case. You may want to park your heavier bags with the hotel bell captain (and leave them a tip when you reclaim). You may or may not be sharing a room with another crew member. You will be allotted a per diem for food, usually dinner and breakfast from the hotel restaurant, and have a chance to hang out with your fellow shipmates. But don't chat too late and get some sleep; it's going to be a long day tomorrow. Depending on which time zone you left, you may be dead on your feet already.

Early the next morning (often around 7:00–8:00 a.m. local time), you will be picked up and shuttled to the port. You are responsible for bringing your own bags (carry-it-all-yourself-in-one-trip again) and will wait in the port terminal for a representative from the Human Resources office. This may take a while as these folks are very busy on a turnaround day. Watch for someone wearing a uniform with stripes on their shoulders or coat sleeves. With clipboard or tablet in hand, they will check your name off the new crew boarding list and escort you onboard. Drag yourself and your gear up the metal gangway. Here you go! (See why you might wanna keep it light?) Depending on location and tides, that gangway is most probably at ground level with easy access—or maybe not.

Once onboard, you will pass through a security check, much like that at the airport. Tuck the phone and electronics from your pockets into a bag. Lift your gear onto the x-ray machine belt, and they will be sure you are not carrying any of the banned items (remember the no-nos).

Security Story

It's funny to see what people try to bring on a cruise. Security agents, for both guests and crew, are looking primarily for alcohol, extension cords/power strips, candles (never, never an open flame onboard) or other fire hazards, weapons, and clothing irons. Confiscated items are given a claim ticket and returned when you sign off at the end of the contract. There is a reclaim table when the guests disembark, and once, I couldn't believe my eyes—on a seven-day cruise, someone brought a Crock-Pot! Were they planning to cook? Crazy folks!

Once you're through security, you will park your gear in a vacant corner, so take your carry-on with you to have passport and medical forms handy. You will be escorted by the HR rep to the medical facility (if not preapproved.) These folks mean *serious business*, and you must supply them with *all* the forms they need. They will scrutinize your info and determine whether you are to be granted approval. They will make copies for their files and return the originals to you. Your medical is valid for two years, so keep it in a *safe* place; you know how much it cost you to have done, and it is your ticket to your next contract, and the next.

Whew! Congratulations, Medical has deemed you an official crew member! Someone from your department will appear to welcome you aboard and show you around. From Medical, you will go to Human Resources to get your crew ID. Your passport will be held in their office, and you won't get it back except for immigration procedures or signing off the ship.

You will receive a plain magnetized access card for your assigned cabin; that is your cabin key. Remember the number; for security, it is not on the card! You will be escorted through the labyrinth of corridors to where you will live. *Try* to remember the path you took to get there! All the hallways will look alike. There will be twists and turns, and there may be stairs involved, so chances are you will get lost often for the first week or so. Keep in mind that on some ships, there is no elevator to the lower crew corridors. This means, of course, dragging those heavy bags down a metal stairway—*ew!* When you sign off, you will have to get it all back up top, and trust me, there will be more than when you came!

On lower decks, some hallways will be blocked by water-tight doors (the big yellow and black-striped ones) that are sometimes open in port and then closed when sailing (you will learn more about those in crew training) or irregular interior hallways. Try to take note of signage on the walls, decorations, posters, etc. to give you clues. Just remember your cabin number so hopefully, you can find your way home later. The ship is a maze; don't beat yourself up if you have to ask directions for a while (yes, guys, you may need to ask for directions!).

HR will also give you an emergency card which will have a number that indicates your duties and responsibilities. This may be red, green, blue, or white and will be an indication of which drills in which you are expected to participate. There is a massive chart in the hallway of the main corridor (called the "I-95" on American ships, the "M-1" on European ones as it is the major "highway" onboard) where your number is listed with its associated emergency role. The guide will briefly describe your duties, which will be elaborated upon later by the safety officer. You will then be given a brief orientation of the ship. You will see the crew mess where your meals will be available. Take note of the open hours there. Some larger ships will have a small portion of the mess available 24–7; others will close between meals. Remember, you are not allowed to take food out of the mess. There is also a slop chest where you can purchase snacks and sundries, but you may have to ask other crew members for directions as it can sometimes be located in odd places. Take a picture of the sign here, too, for open hours, as they may fluctuate depending on itinerary. A crew bar can supply your beverage of choice, usually open in the evenings.

WORK AT SEA, SEE THE WORLD: AN INSIDER'S SECRETS TO THE WORKING LIFE ON A CRUISE SHIP

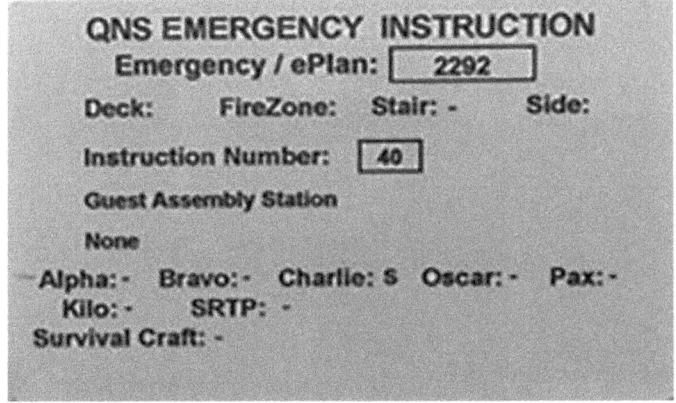

You will be shown your muster station (where you are to report in an emergency or a drill), and you will have a brief safety orientation. In your crew training, you will be taught when and where to go for various situations, but as of your first day, before your ship leaves the dock, you will be required to report to this location and be checked off a list to acknowledge that you are accounted for and know where to go. The codes on your emergency card will indicate in which drills you will need to participate, and they will be explained in training.

You will be taken to the training room; especially remember where this place is! You will be required to participate in eighty hours of classes/activities, and *you* will be responsible for getting yourself there *on time* for each session. Never give any lip to the training officers; those stripes carry a lot of weight, and backtalk and wisecracks can have immediate and dire consequences. (Stories to come.) Guest interaction on an intimate level is also a huge no-no and is sometimes referred to as "chicken or beef," referring to the choice the airline hostess used to offer you on that immediate flight home. There are cameras everywhere—don't even think about it!

If a uniform is part of your job, you will be taken to the distribution locker to collect what is necessary. Some companies will supply them, while others require you to purchase them. Either way, you must provide your own shoes, and required style/brand will be advised prior to your departure from home. After your ship tour, you will be taken back to your luggage and may (or may not) be assisted in getting yourself established in your cabin. You might meet your roommate (if you have one), and you have to squeeze yourself and your stuff into the space available. You should find clean linens and towels ready, but you will probably have to make your own bed.

There are nautical terms which will be explained in more detail in training. But if you're not a sailor, they may be new to you, and some are just fun to know and will make you look like you know what's up right from the start (the **bold** ones are important.)

Port—The left side of the ship when facing forward. It's easy to remember when you realize that "left" and "port" both have four letters, and that is indeed where it is! Marked with a red light at night. Your emergency card may be red, indicating your drill participation on the portside of the ship.

Starboard—The right side of the ship when facing forward; usually marked with a green light at night. That way oncoming vessels can tell if you are coming or going. If you carry a green emergency card, drills will be called for that side.

Forward—Duh! The front of the ship.

Aft—Yep, the rear of the ship.

At anchor—When the ship is tethered to the bottom with a plough-like iron anchor on a chain. If your cabin is anywhere near the bow on lower decks, you will definitely hear the clanking of chains and grinding of winches when it's going up and down when needed.

Azipod—The rotating propeller (if equipped therewith) mounted in the stern that drives the ship. Instead of using a drive shaft, this thing can literally steer the ship sideways or in circles as it rotates.

Berth—The slip where the ship is assigned to dock.

Boat—Typically a lifeboat. Never confuse a boat with a ship; you can put a boat on a ship, but never a ship on a boat. You work on a ship; the boats are those little guys hanging on the sides (the ones *Titanic* was short of, sorry, Jack).

Bow—The actual front of the ship's hull.

WORK AT SEA, SEE THE WORLD: AN INSIDER'S SECRETS TO THE WORKING LIFE ON A CRUISE SHIP

Bow thruster—Propellers mounted in the side of the ship's hull that drive the ship sideways at the bow to push it right or left to maneuver efficiently, mostly used in docking.

Brass monkey—Okay, you don't need to know this, but it's just funny. There is a nautical phrase, "it's cold enough to freeze the balls off a brass monkey." Back in the days of sailing ships, a brass monkey was a metal frame used to hold cannon balls. Low temperatures would cause the frame to contract more than that of the iron balls and might allow them to roll off the frame, hence the term. No relation to jungle animals.

Bridge—The pilothouse at the front of the ship where the captain and navigational officers work to allow full view of the ship to maneuver it both when underway (moving) and docking. They have cameras for visibility on many parts of the ship; they know everything that's happening—yes, everywhere!

Brig—You don't wanna have to go there! It's where the "prisoners" or delinquent crew (or guests) may be housed awaiting debarkation. As an alternative, the offender may be confined to their cabin and a security officer posted outside so everyone knows that something bad happened!

Bulbous bow—I just like the sounds of this term, and nearly all ships are now built with this large rounded protrusion that sticks out below the waterline on the bow. It reduces drag and increases speed, range, fuel efficiency, and stability. You will see a painted drawing of it on the bow to make it apparent to warn small craft not to get too close.

Bunkering—When the ship is attached to a large barge that provides fueling. Never smoke on deck when this process is underway! Potential kaboom!

Cabin—Usually used as a term for crew quarters; *stateroom* more often used for guest rooms.

Captain—The Big Cheese, the master of the vessel and all who sail therein (that means you!)

Captain's daughter—Another unnecessary term but amusing, referring to the cat-o'-nine-tails (a whip made of strips of leather) which was only used at the captain's order for flogging. Ew! It was also kept in a baize bag, a possible origin for the term "the cat's out of the bag" and the reference to a small space as "not enough room to swing a cat." Sometimes a sailor was bent over the barrel of a cannon for a beating with the cat-o'-nine-tails for punishment, and that was called "kissing the captain's daughter." Glad those days are past! On the other hand, don't get caught actually kissing the captain's daughter, or else—cameras, remember?

Clear—Being cleared refers to customs and immigration legalities that are performed by port officials before anyone can get off the ship. You will hear announcements as to when it's over, and you are cleared to go ashore.

Course—The direction and plotted itinerary of the ship.

Deck—The levels of the ship, unlike a building with floors.

Dry dock—Also referred to as a shipyard where vessels go for repair and refurbishment to provide access to the hull. The ship is floated in, put on concrete blocks, and the water is drained out. Wet dock is a slip in the shipyard where the ship stays moored instead of being hauled out. Huge cranes lift containers of equipment onboard, and numerous contractors come onboard.

Engine control room—You may get to see this area in training, as it is where the engineers keep track of all the mechanical operations onboard; they too have cameras, as does the security office. Yep, they're everywhere!

Fair winds and following seas—A maritime blessing for safe journey and good fortune.

Fantail—The aft area of the ship; also known in ancient times as the poop deck (haha, she said poop).

Fathom—Water depth measured by a unit length of about six feet.

Financial Department—The office of those in charge of paychecks and any onboard expenses you incur.

Following seas—Winds are behind the ship, enabling faster headway and a smoother ride.

Galley—The ship's kitchen; one or more for crew, several for guests.

Gangway—Where you get on and off the ship; location may vary with docking system and tides.

WORK AT SEA, SEE THE WORLD: AN INSIDER'S SECRETS TO THE WORKING LIFE ON A CRUISE SHIP

GPS—Just like on land, the navigational system; Global Positioning System.

HR—Human Resources Department; your go-to for cabin issues and other onboard concerns.

Knots—Units of nautical speed; 1 nautical mile is equivalent to about 1.15 miles per hour. Derived from the ancient system of measurement with actual knots tied in a rope that was played out to measure speed.

Landlubber—What you are before you go to sea or after your contract is over.

Lee side—The side of the ship that is sheltered from the wind. Tender boats are launched from the lee side to protect them from the swell and waves on the windward side.

Liberty—The time allowed for crew to go ashore; also called shore leave.

Lifeboat—Really? You need an explanation here? Watch the movie *Titanic* if you do.

Life raft—Where you may end up floating after an extreme emergency; the thing you have to maneuver in training (see chapter 10).

Life jacket—That big orangey yellow thing in your cabin taking up half your closet space (that might save your life or hopefully only be necessary for an occasional safety drill). Sometimes also called a Mae West, named for the actress from the 1930s best known for her large bosom.

Loose cannon—An irresponsible or reckless person whose behavior endangers others. Historically a loose cannon on deck, not adequately secured, weighing thousands of pounds, would crush anything and anyone in its path, maybe breaking a hole in the ship's hull, endangering its seaworthiness.

Mariner—You!

Mess—Not what you left in your room but where you go to eat onboard.

Midships—The middle of the ship, generally halfway between fore and aft; usually the most stable area, especially in a storm.

Moor—To tie the ship to a dock with mooring lines (those massive ropes). The wooden U-shaped boards tethered to the mooring lines are to keep critters from scampering onboard.

Muster drill—An exercise conducted by the crew of the ship, prior to sailing, for the instruction of passengers on safety and emergency procedures. After 2020, some of this may be instructed via TV and apps but still involves physically locating and checking in at your actual station location.

Muster station—Or assembly station; your assigned gathering location for emergency and drill.

Nautical mile—A measurement of distance equivalent to 1,852 meters, 6,076 feet, or 1.151 land miles.

Overboard—Anything tossed off the vessel (major no-no!). Anything or anyone may never be recovered.

Paymaster or purser—The officer responsible for your paycheck in the financial office.

Pilot—Not the one flying the plane but rather an especially knowledgeable person taken aboard to navigate with the captain through specific or difficult waters.

Pitch—The movement of the ship sailing over waves, causing the fore and aft ends to rise and fall repeatedly.

Porthole—If you are lucky enough to have one in your cabin, whoo-hoo! A round window with a metal protective hatch for severe weather protection on lower decks. Can't be opened, but at least you can see out.

Radar—Electronic celestial navigational tool; an acronym for radio detection and ranging. Underwater imaging of obstacles is sonar (sound navigation and ranging).

Raft—That thing in which you may be floating if the ship goes down, but not likely!

Rescue boat—A fast boat launched by a special team for use in case of emergency, especially for man overboard. One on each side of the ship.

Roll—The side-to-side motion of the ship from winds, waves, or swells that rocks you to sleep.

Safe harbor—A protected harbor that provides safety from bad weather.

Scullery—Where the crew goes to deposit food waste and leave dishes for washing.

Ship over—When a crew member chooses to extend their service another term; re-enlist.

Slop chest—Ship's store for sale of merchandise for the crew; sundries and snacks.

Square meal—Meals on sailing ships used to be served to the crew on square wooden planks.

Stabilizer—A wing-shaped structure that can be extended from the side of the ship's hull to smooth the ride in rough seas.

Tender—A boat used for transportation of people and supplies from an anchored ship.

Three sheets to the wind—A sailor who has drunk strong spirits beyond his capacity; not what you ever want to be—the consequences are disastrous!

Wake—The turbulent water aft created by the movement of the ship.

Whitecaps—The foam or spray on wave tops created by strong winds.

Xebec or zebec—Only included for you scrabble freaks; a Mediterranean sailing ship of the sixteenth to nineteenth centuries.

Zulu—Also for scrabble (double or triple letter/word score!); a Scottish fishing boat, and the military call sign for Z or zed.

Sources

Naval Slang Dictionary (pdf).
Hope, Ranger. 2007. *A Seaman's Dictionary.*
Art of Rigging 1848.
Mayne, Richard. 2000. *The Language of Sailing.*
Glossary of Nautical Terms; Practical Boat Owner 2014.
Martin, Gary. 1939. "Let the cat out of the bag"—the meaning and origin of this phrase. *Oxford English Dictionary.* Oxford University Press.

CHAPTER 9

Welcome Aboard!

You are ready to sail. Your new adventure has begun at last, and it will change your life in many ways. Enjoy the ride, and try to keep your enthusiasm, sense of flexibility, and cooperation. Onboard you will find out where you are allowed to go and what sort of wardrobe is expected for various areas. FYI, as a crew member, be aware that there are certain places you are not allowed unless it's your workplace. For example, the navigational bridge, the engine room, and you can't sit in guest bars or (spoiler alert) play in the casino.

Your New "Home"—Cabin Info

Some crew members are allowed a solo cabin, such as officers, department heads, some entertainers, engineers, and security staff that have night shifts. Everyone else is most often assigned to share a cabin with someone of the same sex from your own department. If you are boarding as a couple, you can apply to share a cabin; however, this may still involve bunk beds (but has more floor space than the one-bed arrangement). If your ship has the option of a single share, your space will be even smaller, more like a broom closet with a fold-down bunk. You have the luxury of your own very small space, but you share a bathroom with the adjacent cabin. You can find videos on YouTube that have been posted by crew members to give you a better visual than I was afforded. Accommodations will vary with the company and the ship.

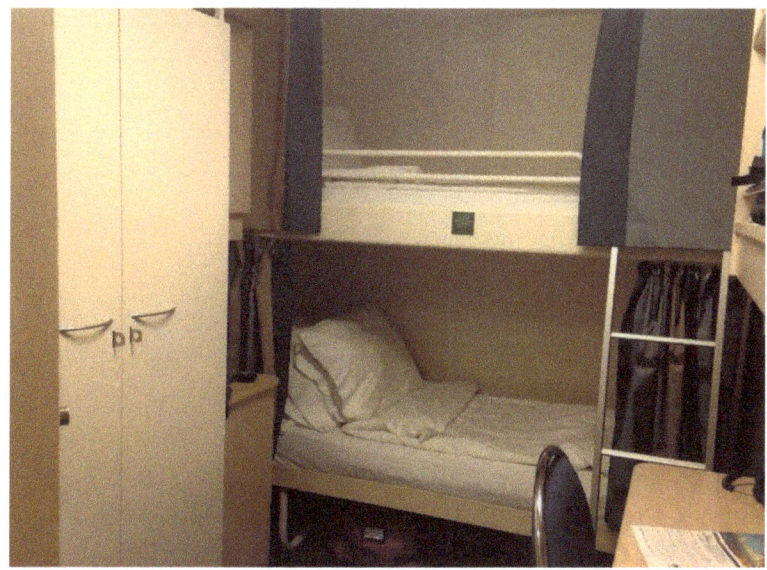

A typical double-crew cabin

The Bunk

The cabin is often as wide as a twin bed is long, and two of them are stacked on a metal frame. Access to the top is via a vertical three-rung metal ladder welded to the side of the bed. The mattresses are firm, often coated in plastic on a corrugated metal slab. Under the bed is often the only place to store luggage, so beware that this space may be only about eleven inches high.

If you live on the top bunk, sometimes the air conditioner/air circulation is mounted on the ceiling and emits a constant *whishing* sound. There is a thermostat in each cabin, but hot air rises, and the cooling air may be shot right at you. There are drapes on each of the bunks, and they provide both privacy and temperature adjustment. You can regulate the heat and light—open a little, close a little, etc. The florescent hall lights that burn 24–7 may spill some night-light from around the entry door, so use the sleep mask if necessary and earplugs—nearly everyone snores sometimes, maybe you?

And maneuvering from the top bunk with occasional rough seas can make for a nocturnal adventure of hazardous proportions; just be careful. There are many circumstances where solid upper-body strength is required on a ship (see the notes on doors), and this is one of them. Be sure to put a chair at the base of the ladder for better footing. It's advisable to go up frontward, and down backward.

The Closet

Your closet/wardrobe is typically only fourteen inches wide and may have two or three six-inch-high drawers below the hanging space. My closet was completely empty upon arrival, but after asking for directions several times, I found my way down to the main laundry, in the depths of the ship, on deck 0, for spare hangers. In unpacking, I realized that, yes, indeed, I had overpacked! There are also the two bulky neon life jackets to accommodate. Be sure they get parked somewhere easily accessible.

Television

Your TV will be an indication of the age of the ship and its upgrades. My first ship had an old TV/VHS combo! You will usually find a flat screen, either on a pivoting wall mount or bolted to a table or desk. The larger ships may have a TV mounted at the foot of each bunk! When I was sailing, however, they had not installed headphone jacks in these, so it might be challenging when you want to watch a blow-up-everything spy movie, and your roomie wants to watch a soppy rom-com; perhaps that has been addressed by now. Also there is often a crew movie channel where you can choose from a selection of free films, so there is no shortage of stuff to help you chill out.

There are a few broadcast channels itemizing onboard activities, port shopping, shore excursions, the various other ships and their routes to entice guests to book their next adventure, and something for the teens and kids. The cruise director usually hosts a morning show where you will get a rundown of the day's activities, some weather info, etc. The ship has contracts with various networks, so the news channels may vary, and there are usually some international sports, ESPN, or Red Bull TV. Depending on the satellite connections, there could be MSNBC, BBC, FOX, or whichever organization with which your company has contracted. At sea, there may be periodic freezes of picture as satellites realign. The TV programs often repeat the same episode over and over and over, and news channels seem to have the same ads over and over and repeat the news. Granted, you will want to just chill out after work or on downtime, and the size of the ship may determine your options. That's where your own hard drive and laptop of entertainment options come in handy.

A Cooler

There may be a flop-down table on wall hinges or a small desk which also houses a bar cooler to keep beverages and such. Not really a refrigerator, it's a cool place for your drinks. Pick up a few snack items in port for those times you just need a nosh, especially on turnaround days when the crew mess may be cleaned up by about 9:00 a.m. Coming back from ports, you will see crew members toting big bags of chips and sodas etc. as their comfort food. You're not allowed to take any food out of the mess, and inspections are held periodically to be sure there is nothing molding or infesting the ship.

The Bathroom

Small is an understatement. A tiny sink nestled in the corner with a double medicine cabinet mounted to the ceiling. I could just see from the top of my head to my nose! I carry a suction-cup attached magnifying mirror to extend the mirror down a bit. The only power plug is reserved for razors alone (if you can reach it!). Hair dryers, curling irons, hot rollers are about the only other electrical heat-related appliances allowed. The other plugs are outside the bathroom, usually both US-spaded plug outlets and European-rounded plugs, but a three-way expander or a multi-USB hub are helpful when you need to share those few plugs for phone charging etc. You might need an adapter or a converter depending on your country of origin.

Phone

There may be direct-access buttons, or you can get a small booklet of department phone numbers from HR to contact various offices. To call off-ship from your cabin phone, you need a calling card, for sale onboard in $10 and $20 denominations. Ask HR where to purchase these. There is usually a Cellular at Sea service that will pop up on your phone, but the rates are high. A local international travel SIM card is a way to avoid astronomical phone charges. Consider before you go whether your cell carrier is appropriate for your travel itinerary. That was on your prep list, right? Most of the time, it's advisable to keep your phone in airplane mode unless you have service in the port where you are.

Onboard Challenges

Besides the minute cabins, there are other ship-design elements that create challenges:

1. Whereas the guest hallways are nicely carpeted, the crew areas are nearly all metal or linoleum flooring. The I-95 is the main thoroughfare for trolleys from galley to dining areas, transporting foodstuffs from one end of the ship to the other. Navigating it requires appropriate footwear.
2. Again the guest areas and stairs are carpeted, but crew stairs are metal, much shallower, and often much steeper. They are built for potential massive quick evacuation. Always use the handrails!

3. Doors come in several different configurations:

   a. Cabin doors usually have an automatic closer, and if you suddenly realize you've locked your key inside, oops! Find your roommate or call security. You may have to go to their office and sign a form to confirm your access before they will let you in.
   b. There are heavier doors that open onto the I-95 from adjacent cabin corridors. Be careful opening these, as there is usually lots of traffic on the other side, day and night. Trying to open these in heels sometimes made me feel like the old cartoon characters with their feet scrambling madly on ice.
   c. Some areas can be closed off by giant sliding fire doors that have a mechanical release-and-track mechanism that beeps when in motion. These are often closed on debarkation days to channel traffic off the ship or closed in actual emergencies to compartmentalize the decks.
   d. Hinged fire doors are barriers between smaller areas and are very heavy. They are usually not to be left open, but when they are, the only way to close them is to release the giant magnet from a switch high on the wall. Occasionally for a drill, these doors can all be remotely closed from the ship's bridge or the control room. Be sure they are never blocked.
   e. Roller fire doors may not be as obvious, as they are built into the structure and decor and built to roll down to close off large areas.
   f. Watertight doors are the beasts! Below decks, there is a massive arrangement of doors that compartmentalize the ship into sections. Should there be an occasion where water or smoke gets into these areas, it can be contained to prevent a *Titanic* situation. These doors are massively heavy, mounted on a track, and controlled by a lever on either side of the door. They are

bright yellow with diagonal black stripes and, if closing, will not stop *for anything*! You must get permission from the bridge to open them. A loud bell rings whenever they are moving. You will find out more about these in training. Often they are open while in port but closed when sailing, so you will find yourself backtracking to a stairwell, going back up to another level to try to find your way across to another section to go back down another stairwell to get where you are going! Welcome to the maze!

So once you figure out how to maneuver around the ship, you will get better at gauging how much time you need to get where you want to go. Welcome to your new home away from home. Get to know your neighbors, enjoy the occasional cabin party if they are allowed. You're on your way to new adventures with new friends.

CHAPTER 10

What's All This About Trainings and Drills?

Okay, what's all this talk about training? What am I being trained for? Well, you think you're here to be a fill-in-the-blank job—wrong! That may be your job title, but you are really here to be part of a massive team of rescue workers. For this, you are required to complete eighty hours of training in various aspects of ship life. There will be lectures, tests, and some actual hands-on exercises that each company may handle in a different way, but the essence is the same. You were issued that emergency card and assigned a safety number that dictates your role in an emergency.

A ship is a very vulnerable entity that is sometimes at the mercy of various elements, be it unexpected storms, careless people who toss a cigarette overboard (which can blow back onto the ship and start a fire—yes, it's been done more than once), galley workers who may lose control of a deep fat fryer, a guest who may have a medical emergency, another ship that may collide with yours in high winds, or even a situation where you need to assist in a rescue of people lost at sea. There are numerous scenarios that have all been thought through completely for handling every one of them (and folks have been sailing since forever), so you are responsible for being a part of the resolution team. At some point in every cruise, each ship will have regular drills enacted to facilitate the smooth and automatic nature of emergency reactions so should there be an *actual* emergency, reaction will be effective and efficient. The color of your emergency card and the codes on it will dictate which drills you are required to attend.

The completion of those eighty hours of training will be required within the first three weeks of arrival. You will be issued certificates at the completion of each segment. *Never lose* these certificates! If you should transfer to another cruise line, or you are called into a class you have already completed, you need these to prove your completion. Some are stored on a computer but only for one company. If you don't have the paper, you may be doing them all over. Some only have to be completed once (providing you have your certification), while others require periodic renewal. Even if you're a rehire, there is always something that will provide new information, and every ship is a bit different from the last! Trainings will include such subjects as fire safety, evacuation procedures, sexual harassment, crowd control, drug and alcohol abuse, behavior guidelines, and company policies, among many others.

Training Story 1

One wise-guy British dancer mouthed off to the training officer on one of the big ships. In spite of the pivotal lead role he was to play in a production show (for which he had spent months rehearsing), the officer told him to pack his bags, and he was off at the next port, at his own expense! This threw the entire theater schedule into a tizzy with orchestra rehearsals changed, cries to the agents to send an immediate replacement, costume refits put on hold, show openings delayed, etc. The ripple effect for such behavior is tremendous. You cannot be rehired once dismissed—you are fired forever! Don't shoot yourself in the foot before you even get started!

Training Story 2

On another ship, there were two Chinese girls from the food service department who obviously were not very fluent in English. One must be able to respond in an emergency situation where information and immediate action are essential. Every time the trainer made a joke in an attempt to enliven a rather dry subject, the girls sat deadpan. By the next training session, they were nowhere to be seen. It can happen that fast. Respect is the key word here. Respect for the offices, respect for the officers, and respect for the system which has been developed for the safety of everyone onboard. They are *very* serious about this information as understanding and acting on it correctly could be the difference between life and death!

Some emergency situations are announced over the public address system with codes so as not to alarm the guests. If there is a small galley flare-up that needs attention, there is no need to publicly cause a mass panic announcing fire when it is not necessary! Only the relevant resolution team need be notified up front. Some of the codes you will hear announced (and learn about) include the following:

1. ***Alpha*** *(medical alert)*—Should anyone become injured or ill, you will learn who to call and what to do that could save a life. There is a full medical team onboard, but basic CPR procedures will be covered. If a person has fallen down the stairs, what to do. If a person is choking or having an allergic reaction in the dining room, what to do until the medical team can arrive. First aid and survival techniques are addressed that can save lives.

    Story: I was once the person they called to rescue! I was singing with my band in a lounge, and suddenly, I heard my ears ringing, and I fainted onstage. I wasn't out for long, and when I came around, the medical team was there picking me up. I was wheelchaired down to the medical facility for assessment and care. It was encouraging that they were so Johnny-on-the-spot. I was fine except for the embarrassment and the surprise. I was just dehydrated, and there was no further cause for alarm. *Remember to drink lots of water!*

2. ***Bravo*** *(fire)*—Fire is the most dangerous hazard onboard. Not only because of the flames but also injury or death from the smoke. You will learn how to raise the alarm, what to do, where to go, how to determine the cause, and the dif-

ferences between various fire extinguishers, where to find them, what they are for, and how to use them efficiently.

Fire story: As part of a training exercise, I was suited up as one of the fire team, with the whole outfit, air tank, and helmet. The mask was covered with back fabric inside, simulating what it would be like if you couldn't see due to massive smoke. We were then told that someone had passed out in a corridor down one deck, and we were to go and find them and get them out. When you suddenly can't see, you forget that you can still hear and touch! Getting used to an air tank (like a scuba diver), the feeling was very claustrophobic, and I could hear myself breathing! Once we had calmed down, we formed a line with hands on the shoulder of the one in front of us and realized that we could actually talk to each other! We felt our way down the hallway to the stairs and passed the information back about where we were going, where the stairs were to feel for the steps with our feet, and where the person was that we found under the stairs. Again, talking to one another, we found the "body" and determined how we could best lift him out of the situation. Together we retraced our steps back up to fresh air. It was a real-life experience in awareness of how the actual fire team will manage in a real emergency.

Smoke story: Another exercise was staged such that a corridor was flooded with smoke, and we had to feel our way through to escape. Staying as low as possible, talking to one another, feeling for walls and doors, watching for emergency lighting was a taste of the processes for emergency escape. While trying to cover nose and mouth to prevent smoke inhalation, we had to make our way down steps, through a labyrinth of corridors, and back up another set of stairs to the fresh air.

Fire Hose Training: Have you ever handled an actual fire hose? A mooring deck hatch will be opened in the side of the ship. A full-size fire hose will be unreeled, and you will learn to handle this monster. This is a three-person job. One holds the nozzle, another stands behind in a wide stance to brace the first, and the third mans the valve. The object of the game is to get the spray out through the hole—be prepared to get wet! That thing has a helluva kick, and the power is awesome! It was my favorite part of training!

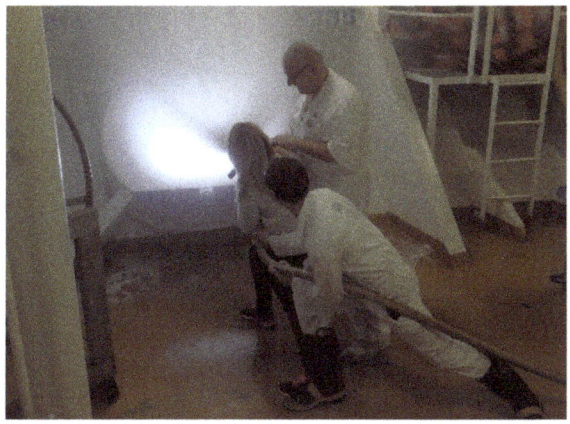

3. ***Charlie*** *(bomb threat/suspicious person)*—If you hear "Charlie…Charlie…Charlie" announced, you may be required to search for "the bomb." It may be a plain brown-wrapped package with the words bomb written on it, or just an unidentified backpack. If you find it, *do not touch it* and instead report its location to the bridge by phone. One crazy guy found it and proudly put it on the safety officer's desk with a "Look what I found!" Oops! I have also seen it enacted with a "suspicious person" recruited to be questioned and identified. An exercise in awareness.
4. ***Delta*** *(damage to the ship)*—Possible biohazard, fuel barge issues, etc. *No smoking!* Fire team will respond.
5. ***Echo*** *(drift/potential collision/high winds at port)*—You might have seen YouTube footage of a collision between two Carnival ships a few years ago in high winds in Mexico. It happened in full view of other docked ships, and the bow of one ship was literally raked through the stern dining room of the other one. How unnerving for the captains, not to mention expensive! Winds can be erratic and dangerous. No one was injured, but it was an alert to the unpredictable nature of the weather.
6. ***Kilo*** *(report to your emergency station)*—Yep, if you're still in bed, get your butt into some pants and get to your station, pronto! Announced both in drills and emergencies.
7. ***Oscar*** *(person overboard)*—It is impossible to "fall" overboard. Railings, windows, and open decks are all well designed to protect the passengers. However, cruise ship vacations create an interesting dynamic among people. There may be massive amounts of alcohol consumed, people living in small spaces, families that do not often hang together are assembled for a family event, and conflict can occur. A person may actually choose to attempt to end their life, and jumping overboard may seem like an answer to their dilemma.

   Story 1: A seventy-seven-year-old man had just had a disagreement with his family and, in broad daylight, had climbed the aft railing outside the buffet area. A crew member saw him and immediately came to his aid and, grasping his hand on the rail, calmly talked to him about what he was doing. The passenger finally softened in his determination, and other crew members quietly approached to assist. When the man had calmed down, he was persuaded to come back inside, and the others helped him back over the rail to safety. The crew members were subsequently rewarded for their efforts by the captain and publicly acknowledged for their care and quick thinking. The man subsequently wrote a very long apology letter to the captain, thanking him profusely for the attentiveness and kindness of the crew and expressing his appreciation for their quick thinking by saving him from a really disastrous mistake.

Story 2: In the Caribbean, we were awakened at 2:00 a.m. by the call of *"Oscar...Oscar...Oscar!"* A man had argued with his partner amid some heavy drinking and had jumped overboard from his cabin balcony. As it was a large ship, he had landed toward the aft end of a lifeboat below. As he hung there, security was summoned immediately, and help was dispatched. But in his inebriated state, the man had shouted to his partner above, "I'm doing this because of you!" After which he literally let go and fell into the ocean. The rescue boat was dispatched, and we stayed in the area for over an hour until the US Coast Guard took over the search. As far as I know, he was never found. The undertow of a ship underway makes it nearly impossible to avoid being sucked under the hull. The ship cannot stop on a dime! Not a happy way to go, and the wake (so to speak) of such actions leaves a trail of tears, bewilderment, and anxiety. Be aware of people's mental state and take care. You will learn some important identifying factors and support techniques in training to help others. We all have occasional bad days; look out for each other!

8. *Papa*—Environmental emergency such as an oil or fuel spill.
9. *Zulu*—Fight onboard (on some ships), and security is dispatched immediately.

Other trainings may include the following:

A. *Crowd control*—At boarding for every cruise, some crew members will be assigned to man the muster stations. Selected assembly areas of the ship are designated to which guests will report in an emergency. The drill for all guests (commonly called PAX drill) must occur according to maritime law before the ship sails. Associated duties include manning stairwells, directing guests to their appropriate station, checking them in, and demonstrating the proper wearing of a life jacket. Skills will be taught on how to manage people, obtain assistance in an emergency from others, and how to control a crowd as best as can be done in an actual emergency situation.
B. *Drugs*—The essence of this training is to make everyone aware that illicit drug use of any kind will *not* be tolerated. All the secrets are revealed on how others have attempted to hide their stash and the consequences when it is *always* discovered. There is a zero-tolerance policy at sea, and any infringement will result in (a) immediate dismissal, (b) confinement under guard, (c) disembarkation at the current port in handcuffs, and/or (d) incarceration by the local authorities, and/or (e) loss of any opportunity for future employment. In essence, it's the training warning that says, "Just don't even think about it!" You absolutely cannot fool a sniffing dog!
C. *Sexual harassment*—This is a serious issue when so many people live in close proximity, often under stressful situations. The need is emphasized (and enforced) for mutual respect of all persons regardless of age, nationality, gender, or sexual orientation. Any unwelcome advances are

to be respected without question, and those who persist in aggressive behavior are subject to disciplinary action. In other words, behave yourself and respect everyone.

D. *Lifeboat and evacuation procedures*—At some point in every cruise, there will be a crew safety drill. They are usually held when docked in a port where most of the guests have left the ship. Your colored emergency card will indicate if you are involved. No shore leave will be permitted until your assigned drill is complete. It usually entails checking in at your muster station and enacting your assigned duties. This may take anywhere from one hour to three, depending on the extent of the drill.

Periodically those crew assigned to a lifeboat may be required to don the life jacket and hard hat and board the boat. It is then lowered to the water (without guests) to be driven around, checking the maintenance and operating condition, as well as the commander's piloting skills. You will learn the list of survival equipment provided onboard: water, dehydrated food, fishing gear, flares, lights, etc. A periodic coast guard inspection will test you on this list. For those assigned to a raft, you will learn about the procedures for getting off the ship while at sea. This can be in the form of cables and pulleys, or chutes that you slide down. The procedures relevant to your particular ship will be explained.

Evacuation Duties

This includes managing crowds and assisting in evacuation procedures. For example, how would you evacuate a 323-pound older man, from an upper deck, who is confined to a wheelchair? He might be overcome from smoke and can't help you. You can't use an elevator. What to do? This is one of the reasons that English has been established as the common maritime language. Everyone *must* be able to communicate effectively in a wide variety of circumstances. Cooperation and preparedness are essential to efficient procedures in the event of an emergency, whether for one person's benefit or for an entire shipload of over six thousand people in the middle of the ocean (yes, in training you will find out the answer to the big-boy-evacuation dilemma)!

As there is frequent crew turnaround with members signing on or off, the safety officer will determine if it's time to remind the crew about the more extensive actual emergency experience. This drill is always done in a port, preferably without guests aboard. It entails rounding up a number of crew (based on the capacity of the lifeboats on that particular ship), assembling them at various muster stations, attiring them in life jackets, parading them through the ship along an appropriate escape route, and literally loading them into a lifeboat. It is a reality check on how important it is to follow safety measures onboard such that you may *never* have to face this actual possibility. Everything you own will be left behind, and you will be packed like sardines into a floating metal tub—that may or may not have a bathroom! People are assigned a seat in an Escheresque configuration of seats that face each other, stacked atop one another, and every square inch is full of bodies. Just imagine bobbing around an open ocean with possibly three-hundred-plus sweaty anxious people. Some may be claustrophobic, many may become seasick, and heaven help you all if you (or anyone else) have to poop!

The Raft

For emergency evacuation, you may be assigned a raft. You will see large barrels lashed to the decks that house the inflatable rafts. It's questionable whether it is preferable to be stuck in a lifeboat with three-hundred-plus seasick people or floating on an inflatable raft, but those are the options. God forbid you should ever actually have to experience the need for either! It is extremely rare, but there is a process established of necessary preparedness.

Whereas the guests are herded into lifeboats from a deck as mentioned before, the general crew are more likely assigned to a life raft. Those huge barrels are dropped to the water, crew are lowered to the water level via a sort of double-pulley system with harnesses. Some of the huge ships now have a giant zigzag inflatable tube where you slide down instead. Most rafts accommodate about 25 crew members, but some new ones may accommodate up to 150!

To prepare for emergencies, training procedures are enacted either in the ship's pool (when guests are away) or, in some cases, in a port near the dock. Wearing the ever-attractive neon life jacket (with its light and whistle), one has to jump into the water feetfirst, holding the life jacket so that it doesn't knock you in the chin upon entry. If you're in either the pool or the ocean, the salt water helps with the floating. One does not have to know how to swim as the life jacket forces you to float. But I have been amazed at how many people working on the ocean are afraid of the water. If you are, it's okay; there is no danger of drowning in a life jacket. Once others are also in the water, the idea is to connect to one another as quickly as possible. This makes you, as a group, more visible to potential rescuers. Your body is kept easily afloat with the life jacket, so you wrap your legs around another person. You create a chain and make it into a big circle. Hopefully you are in warm waters and help is on the way, or you have a raft to head for!

WORK AT SEA, SEE THE WORLD: AN INSIDER'S SECRETS TO THE WORKING LIFE ON A CRUISE SHIP

The raft dropped from the ship may not land upright. For the drill, once in the water, you must paddle toward a small overturned life raft. You climb from the water onto the top (bottom) of the raft, grab the ropes attached thereto, then leverage your weight at the edge of the raft to pull it over to the right side. Then having been thrown back into the water by the flipping, climb into the opening on the side, get yourself secure, then assist others who are floating around you into the raft. So now you are wet and tucked into a rubber floating cork with other wet, sweaty, and scared crew members! Just hope you are in a warm climate if there is an emergency! I admit that I could not have accomplished this feat without the assistance of the two large galley crew who were already in the pool that gave me a boost up, but I did it (twice, as I did not have my certificate from one cruise line when I went to another and had to repeat it all—I say again, *don't* lose your certificates!)!

There is a plethora of trainings, always providing new safety awareness and instructions you must complete satisfactorily. The chief officer safety *really* wants you to pass! If you don't, and you are sent home, there is a whole lot of paperwork involved, and someone would have to be hired on short notice to fill your position. Attendance for these trainings is mandatory.

Sometimes there may be an all-crew evacuation in a port with everyone filing down the gangway and assembling on the pier in a designated area. Be prepared to be standing in the hot sun for a while as your crew is usually a whole lotta folks, and that will take some time! Take a sun hat and wear comfy shoes.

The first few weeks onboard will be overwhelming, with safety trainings on top of what is necessary for your particular job, so be prepared to be temporarily exhausted. There are periodic all-crew meetings for acknowledgment of achievements and awards. There are also regular solicitations for safety suggestions, so keep your eyes open for anything you deem to be potentially hazardous and report it as requested. Safety is everyone's business! Maintaining the most consecutive days without a mishap is a source of pride for each ship, and there is a digital board to keep track and make the crew aware of it.

But drills keep everyone prepared for whatever emergency potential may arise. You are a pivotal part of the whole ship operation, and it is essential that all the crew members know their duties, cooperate with one another, and become efficient team members for the good of everyone onboard.

Other Duties

Port manning is a rotating system of having someone from every department onboard while the ship is in port should an emergency arise. It is in this instance that you have to be proficient at your particular emergency duty and know who to contact should the occasion arise. This is a serious responsibility that may mean having to forgo lunch at your favorite beach café this time—sorry. If you need to kill time and still be available, there is always laundry.

In the next chapter, you'll find out what really happens in actual everyday life onboard!

CHAPTER 11

What Really Happens Below Decks?

> *A true friend is someone who thinks that you are a good egg even though he knows that you are slightly cracked.*
>
> —Bernard Meltzer

Most often, you will be sharing a cabin with someone usually from your own department. Living in a small space with a strange person can create some challenges. They will be of the same sex, but maybe from another country, have differences in culture and personal hygiene, and speak a different native language. Although fluency in English is required by maritime law (I'll say that again), there may be accents or pronunciations that may be confusing. For instance, in the UK, if they invite you to come by and rap on their door, they might ask you to "come knock me up!" (Perhaps not what you thought they meant.) Some may insist on sleeping in the nude, which you may find alarming—or maybe that's you!

Cohabitation demands that you agree on some parameters: keeping the room cool or hot; sleeping with the TV on or silence; leaving the bathroom light on all night or darkness; crank up the music or rest; one wants to sleep in, the other is an early bird; one wants to retire early, the other may be working until 2:00 a.m.; one hangs their laundry in the shower, when the other wants to use it. There may be differences in religious beliefs, political opinions, or family situations. And again, nearly always, there is somebody who snores. Not sayin' it's you, but…These are all situations that require diplomacy, courtesy, communication, and flexibility. It doesn't hurt to be prepared with a sleep mask and earplugs!

Every day brings opportunities to find a rhythm between yourselves, but talking out the situation is crucial to making it work smoothly. Over all, be considerate of each other's preferences and needs. If issues cannot be resolved between you, talk with your department head. Another roommate may be arranged, or a cabin move may be an option. This is more easily accomplished on a turnaround day (the end of one cruise and the start of another) as there is a constant stream of new sign-ons in most departments. HR can help facilitate a change if need be, given sufficient notice.

Cooperation (yep, that word again) is essential for all onboard. It is an exercise in international relations and often works more efficiently than most governments. Hopefully living in close proximity should give you some insight into other cultures and languages, and create more empathy among people. Go with the flow. Discuss your schedules, arrange times for use of the bathroom or TV time, and be considerate of each other. The following should be common sense, but there are certain cooperative behaviors that are standard etiquette:

1. If your roommate's curtains are closed, that means either (a) I'm here, possibly sleeping, and do not want to be disturbed; or (b) please stay out.
2. If something is not yours, don't touch it. Shampoo, soap, or lotion left in the bath, it's not yours; don't rummage through drawers or closets. "Do unto others as you would have them do unto you" (sound familiar?). Remember those locks if necessary.
3. Be considerate of light and sound. If your roommate is sleeping when you get in late, don't slam doors and closets

and turn on the TV. (Remember the advice about ear plugs and sleep masks.) Communicate regarding schedules.
4. Share the responsibilities for cabin cleanup, especially before the periodic inspections, as it is important to pass! Cleanliness is very important. And at sign-off, your cabin must be left as sanitary as possible; leave it as you would like to find it! Sanitization is essential.

Should you need anything in your cabin repaired, call the facilities department. If your phone doesn't work, go to HR and report it. The telephone is an essential communication device should there be an emergency. You might need to report an issue called the TNF, which means your toilet is not flushing! Plumbing onboard can be a nightmare. The company issues its own brand of toilet paper as the septic system onboard is *very* sensitive. Absolutely *nothing* that you have not already eaten, or small amounts of the tissue, are to be deposited in the plumbing system. Should this advice not be heeded, there may be a sewage backup, and your bathroom, the cabin, and the entire hallway may be overrun with the nastiest stuff you would ever want to see or smell! Your carpet will be ruined (along with anything sitting on it), and even if it gets cleaned up, the smell may last for *ages*! *Yuk!* Don't even think of putting *anything* in that receptacle that doesn't belong there. That sucking-air sound that indicates it has been cleared is a relief.

Toilet joke: Never push the flush button when seated! There was a lady on a cruise in Mexico that did so and got stuck from the suction. She was in a handicap-accessible cabin which had a phone nearby for any emergency. Being embarrassed to be caught with her pants down, she put the big sombrero she had just bought on shore on her lap. The plumber came to her rescue and had to tell her, "Well, madame, you'll be just fine, but I'm afraid the Mexican is a goner!"

I think the two most vital workers are plumbers and those in charge of the air-conditioning! Life would be unbearable without them! Give them the respect they deserve. I have found it doesn't hurt to keep a stash of candy bars on hand for extra appreciation of a job well done if the need should arise for any extra help.

Staying well fed in the crew mess: can you survive healthy? And what if you're vegan?

The crew mess is an adventure in itself! The chefs must accommodate a wide range of preferences from many different countries. As a large number of crew are from Indonesia, India, Philippines, and other southern Asia areas, there is always a plethora of white rice. There are usually two dining areas: the crew mess, and the staff and officers mess. The former is larger and noisier; the latter is for officers or those of rank and has generally similar fare but may have a bit more ambiance and a less noisy atmosphere.

Just a point of trivia, to give you some scope, one of the largest ships, the *Symphony of the Seas*, is feeding about 6,000 guests and 2,200 crew. In seven days, they will go through:

1. 60,000 eggs
2. 9,700 pounds of chicken
3. 15,000 pounds of beef
4. 20,000 pounds of potatoes
5. 700 pounds of ice cream
6. 450 cases of champagne (guest parties and art auctions)!
7. 6 million coffee beans for the 1,500 pounds of coffee
8. 2,100 pounds of lobster tails (guest fare for sure!)
9. 12,600 pounds of flour
10. 2,500 pounds of salmon
11. 5,000 pounds of french fries
12. 5,300 pounds of bacon
13. 12,000 pounds of flour tortillas
14. 2,000 pounds of chicken wings
15. 479,314 gallons of fresh water every day (made onboard)
16. 110,000 pounds of ice to serve that water cold

Much of this list is guest fare, but you can count on a lot of that chicken, beef, and french fries ending up in the crew recipes. So there is a lot of food, but the choices will be varied depending on your itinerary. Fresh produce is often acquired from local sources. If the ethnic foods provided are not to your taste, you have to get creative with what's available. There is always a salad bar and chicken and/or pork in some form. Vegetarians may find the vegetables selection redundant, and one may have to go to special lengths to get some without butter and oil; a vegetarian may be fine, vegans, well, hmm, do the best you can. If there is no port access from which to purchase your own goodies, you may request that the slop chest order nonperishable things on your behalf.

The following suggestions are from my good friend and music director who went vegan several years ago and continues to make ship life work:

> Basically it is going to be difficult to stay 100 percent vegan. Because there are so many East Indians among the crew, there is often some delicious vegetarian curry, but most likely it is made with milk or butter. You can't cook for yourself, and for a while, there may be no access to shore markets. Once that changes, you can bring some things back and store them in your minifridge, but this can get expensive. You will have to check with security as to what is allowed. You may be tempted to snag some fruit from the mess, but it is not allowed in your cabin and can prompt an inspection fail—never a good thing. But generally, you just have to get used to eating whatever is provided. There is a huge variety, and there is most often a salad bar available.

Fitness

There is a well-equipped (often windowless) crew gym for your off-duty use. Depending on your rank and privileges, you may even have off-peak time access to the more extensive guest gym. In the alternative, in the privacy of your own cabin, you may choose to assemble your own portable gym. Put some workout routines on your laptop, tablet, or phone, stick in your earbuds and go for it! You can make weights out of water bottles, use stretchy Pilates bands, and floor discs that work on either hard floor or carpeting. And they all fit in a neat little bag in your luggage.

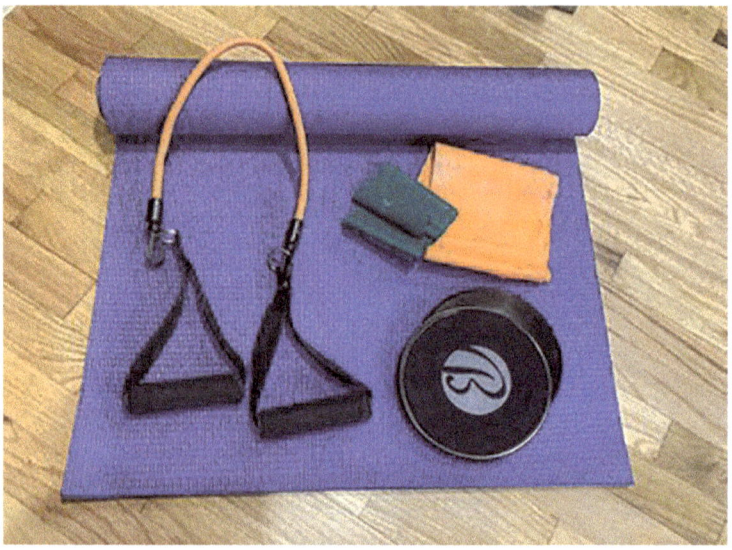

Time Warp

Life onboard will warp your sense of time. One day runs into another. Sometimes you work late and don't even see the light of day. You may have to turn on the TV to find out what time it is and where the hell in the world you are! But with periodic time zone changes, it is essential to keep up with what time it *really* is—remember the analogue clock advice! For now, this is home. Sometimes you may have to check the plaque in the floor of the elevator to confirm what day it is.

WORK AT SEA, SEE THE WORLD: AN INSIDER'S SECRETS
TO THE WORKING LIFE ON A CRUISE SHIP

Finally! I'm in a Relation Ship

Relationships

Are they really true, all those stories about sex below decks? Well, the short answer is yes. Living onboard for so many months, there are indeed opportunities for occasional liaisons with relationship partners, either short-term or potentially long-term. Having come from a no-PDA (public display of affection) in-the-workplace environment, it was initially surprising to me to see hand-holding or an arm draped across another shoulder on the I-95. But here, relationships onboard have been equated to dating in dog years. Everything moves about seven times faster than on land! Sometimes a request is submitted to HR to move in with the new boyfriend after maybe a month of dating. That I-love-you bomb may then lead to the other person signing off in a month, and that's the end of it. But for others, it could be a relationship that may lead to becoming partners for life. Many spouses have been created on ships, but many undeclared spouses may have been left at home, so just beware. You never know who you might meet, as long as you stick to only fellow crew members. This may require some finagling with your roommate for some privacy! I once had a roomie who was visited late at night by a galley worker, and I heard some really interesting sounds outside my curtains! Remember, *any* relations with guests are strictly forbidden and will get you disembarked immediately. Generally the guests are families or couples, but there are the occasional spring breakers who may have conquests on their minds. Or even the seniors: I had a South African friend from the spa who became the obsession of a senior British guest who was determined to take her home. He even went to the Melbourne British Embassy while we were in port to see about getting papers to take her to the UK. Finally the staff captain intervened, much to my friend's relief.

For decades there have been stories about the philandering going on below decks, and the TV show *The Love Boat* (broadcast from 1977–87) and *Below Deck* (2013–) stoked that flame. Yes, it does go on. FYI, pregnancy is a career-changer. You won't be back for another contract. Some people marry, have numerous kids, and live together in one or the other of their countries. They may even (one or both) come back to work once the kid(s) are taken care of by a relative, but that's a tough road. So heed the emphatic advice provided from other crew members—*double condom!* Make such directions in life a choice and not an accident.

> ***Many people will walk in and out of your life, but only true friends will leave footprints in your heart.*** (Eleanor Roosevelt)

Side Jobs—Some Extra Cash

On sea days, there's nowhere to go. If you've got some time off, there are side jobs that provide a way to snag extra cash.

The art gallery is big business for the ships, as they offer an extensive collection of both original artwork, lithographs, serigraphs, and sculptures. Those in charge round up the guests for regular auctions where they educate and sell, and sometimes host the actual artist onboard. For these events (usually incentivized by free-flowing champagne), they need bodies to shuffle the product. There is a display in a gallery area, and a giant locker where additional works are stored. For the auction, the framed works are loaded onto a trolley and rolled to the auction location, usually one of the lounges, where a podium, easels, and lights are set up for preauction perusal. Your job, should you choose to accept it, is to shuffle the artwork on and off the stage for the auctioneer, set aside what has been purchased, and shlep the rest back to the display area or the locker. One must be strong, silent, attentive, helpful, and responsive. It's a little extra cash in your pocket, gives you some exercise, and is a productive and helpful way to kill some time. And you know, you just might learn something about art!

The port shopping team provides another opportunity for extra income. The recommended shops in the ports offer price and quality guarantees for purchasing at these partner stores. In exchange, the ship promotes their patronage. Nearly every port has a Diamonds International, a Cariloha Bamboo clothing, a Del Sol color-changing attire, and a Tanzanite International, to name just a few. To drive people to these locations, the port shopping guide holds a big event in the main theater to explain it all and give out coupons as incentive for bargains. You can assist by distributing coupon books, preparing VIP cards, or handing out shopping maps at the gangway as the guests disembark at the port. It helps out the shopping team and gets you some extra cash for more Wi-Fi or snacks in the slop chest.

Free Time

Yes, it will happen! What to do? Could be a chance to do laundry, work out in the gym, or catch up on sleep. But here are a few other options:

1. *Identify your photos*—If you are a photographer, catalog or identify your plethora of photographs to remember where all the places were that you took those pics. On the advice of a photographer shipmate, take note of the date and location at the gangway and also have a reference for what time

you need to be back onboard that day. It's a huge help in later cataloging photos. You visit many ports repeatedly, so honestly, after a while you can't be sure if that spectacular beach was Nassau or St. Croix!

2. *Watch a movie*—Some ships have free crew-accessible movies available on your cabin TV. Live programming is very limited, and the broadcast team shows the same episodes and news reports over and over and over! I carry a large-capacity external hard drive (at least two or four terabytes) with downloaded movies or TV series onto it, and I always found someone else willing to share their collection. It has definitely expanded my film options; trade if you can to share yours. It helped for storing all those photos, too, to free up space on the phone or camera card!

3. *Read a book!* There is usually both a crew library (sometimes with books in some interesting languages) and a guest library. There are novels, biographies, and art books to be perused. There is no set lending period, so take your time, but be sure to put them back for someone else to enjoy. And contribute your own that you may have brought or purchased when you finish them! COVID precautions removed these libraries (hopefully temporarily), so you might have to supply your own books. Actually I find digital editions the best. Even though you can't share them, you can carry an entire library in your phone! I'm also a fan of audiobooks that allow free hands for other activities.

4. *Journal*—Take the time to record your adventures. These notes will be great reminders later of where you've been, whom you've met, and what you did. The chance to swim with dolphins or bathe with elephants are experiences best captured while they are fresh in your mind. You will have stories from all your adventures, and no doubt someone will want to hear all about them. Expressing your feelings being so far away from home will help you process your emotions.

5. *Language study*—See information in chapter 16 about getting prepared for a foreign country or polishing your English skills.

Crew Bar

Off-duty time in the evening is most often spent in the crew bar. The drink prices are far below what the guests are paying upstairs for the same thing (maybe a beer for $1.50!). The crew bar is usually packed after about 11:00 p.m., when most people are off work. Smokers usually have a designated area, often located on an outside aft deck for ventilation. Be absolutely positive to dispose of smoking materials in the designated secure apparatus and be mindful of others around you.

The crew bar is often the venue for periodic parties that celebrate any country's independence day and may include serving relevant food. The chefs enjoy concocting various ethnic delicacies, and it's a good chance to try something new. In addition, holidays like Easter, Valentine's Day, Thanksgiving, Christmas, Hanukkah, etc. usually prompt decorations and other related festivities. Halloween can be a blast. While you may be making a toga costume out of your bedsheets, others come fully prepared for full-on costuming with makeup and accessories. It's not uncommon to be surrounded by dancing zombies or drag queens in full regalia.

There will always be groups of crew members from the same department (easily identified by their uniforms just off work) and those of same nationalities, as people are anxious to converse in their native languages. This is total chill time, but be mindful of the alcohol-consumption limitations and bug out and get some sleep before the next day's shift. Your health is the most important thing.

A happy crew makes for happy guests, and HR tries darn hard to make living aboard a good experience as best they can. There are DJs, table tennis matches, crew bands that like to jam, lots of karaoke, movie nights, cheese and wine parties, pizza parties, and on and on. Occasionally some of the officers might be serving up custom crepes in the mess, or the captain may even host a waffle-and-ice-cream party on the bridge! HR can also arrange for special excursions for crew in the ports. If your work schedule allows, get out and experience as many of these as you can.

Any excuse, even without a holiday, is a reason for a crew party that nearly always includes bargain prices (if not freebies) on alcohol and sodas. The only major catch here is that the legal limit for anyone is a blood alcohol concentration (BAC) level of no more than *.08*! That's about one beer! And security will not hesitate to breathalyze you should they deem it necessary. Because should there be an emergency, *everyone* needs to be sober and ready to spring into action for the safety of all onboard. Part of your eighty hours of training will be spent discussing the importance of this rule. So just beware. If you have a tendency to overindulge, *don't*. It can easily get you kicked off the ship immediately.

Make an effort to break away from your usual paisanos and try to get to know folks from other departments. It's always good to have a friend in the security department, one among the dining room waitstaff, the tech person, maybe someone in housekeeping, etc. You will be there for months, but everyone is on a different contract schedule. Getting to know folks from other countries may provide a place to hang out on vacation (how about a trip to the Brazil or Slovenia?) with a new friend anxious to share their world.

You will hear so many different languages! There will undoubtedly be names you can't pronounce (ah, the joy of name tags!). Don't be bashful about asking them how to pronounce it or if they have a nickname that you can actually remember (and write them down until you do!). Find ways to discover your commonalities and celebrate your differences. The world seems like a huge place, but the more you travel, the smaller it becomes until you feel like not just a member of your hometown but a citizen of the world. And honestly, we are all human, and we all need the same emotional support system, especially when so far away from home.

CHAPTER 12

Any Special Advice for New Hires?

You've been given a taste of what's in store. Should you decide to embark on this adventure for the first time, what follows are bits of advice from those who have gone before you, from all different companies and departments onboard. You will become a part of a small group that is an integral part of a large team that is a part of a massive corporate structure. But *you* are crucially important in so many ways. Your job is a position that must be filled by someone in the overall structure of the industry. Your ship has a limited number of positions and specific cabin and performance assignments for those fulfilling those positions. The smooth operation of your department, and the overall onboard activity design, can be a virtual house of cards. If you screw up, or become the weak link, the consequences to others can be expansive and expensive. Each and every job comes with tremendous responsibility and an expectation of conscientious behavior, the exercise of common sense, and the necessity for cooperation. On the other hand, because you are so crucial, every effort is made to ensure your safety and well-being.

My five personal bits of advice:

1. Keep an open mind.
2. Be flexible and cooperative.

3. Don't overpack!
4. Save your money.
5. Enjoy the ride!

That said, these are some of the tidbits of advice offered up to any new hire. They are quoted from open Facebook postings representing numerous departments and provided without editing or foreign language corrections.

> Focus on your work, you are onboard to work not to cruise. Working on ships is a big responsibility, so if you don't feel ready for it, don't lie to yourself. On the other hand, it is an environment that will teach you a lot for being exposed to so many different cultures. Be always humble and respect everyone.

> Work more & talk less…Stay away from slackers and ass lickers—otherwise sooner or later you will become like them and you will be angry.

> Oh sh#t, SAVE $$!

> When you live on deck 2 and work is on deck 12, it's a 5-minute commute!

> Be kind and friendly to everyone, no matter what department. We are all human and deserve to be treated with respect! And be proud of who you are!

> Before I joined my friends who worked onboard they told me a lot of information and even with all that…it was nothing of what I expected. I found friends that are more than family now and I also learned so much from the world about

people. Enjoy the diversity and be humble and friendly all the time. You may see your co-workers over and over again across different ships (they might end up being your roommates). Rest, use good shoes and take care of your physical health. Be honest and enjoy yourself. Dance and create memories. If you want a career you can—it is achievable for everyone who works hard and is serious. But if you just want to travel, great... enjoy!

May the Force be with u!!!!

Save your money!! Be flexible, expect the unexpected, don't stress yourself, be respectful, be a diplomat!! If you don't like it, don't stay!

Do not fall in love... (broken heart emoji)

Focus, Learn, Practice, Enjoy. Go out. Make friends. Party hard and most importantly, Trust yourself and Love hard. Ship life is not easy, but it sure is a lot of fun.

Enjoy it. Because the rest will never be the same.

Once you already lost your mind, be brave and enjoy.

Never forget why you chose to work on a cruise ship. Keep the eye on the prize always! Enjoy the pleasures of ship life but don't get carried away.

Watch out for your health. Money is not everything. What's the point of earning all the money in the world, if you lose your health.

WORK AT SEA, SEE THE WORLD: AN INSIDER'S SECRETS TO THE WORKING LIFE ON A CRUISE SHIP

Be on time for f%# sake!

If you survive your first 4–6 months you can survive anything life throws at you!!!

Have fun, don't stress yourself.

You learn 3 things on a ship. PATIENCE, TOLERANCE, AND TEMPER CONTROL TO ITS FINEST. If you can't master this, don't do it.

Stay away from wolves…First contract you are fresh meat for them! (for the girls especially)

Everything is legal until you get caught—don't test them!

Don't bring too many clothes as u cannot wear it, rather bring some snacks from your country!

Download some porn. Because once your there you can't.

Relax, you can make mistakes but make sure nobody knows about it—hahahaha. Forget about finding the love of your life on a ship. Sleep well and eat healthy. Party often but not too much haha. Use condom. Buy at least 10 pairs of socks the same colour before embarking. Don't spend too much on beers.

Be humble, open minded to learn and experience many cultures, habits and the sky is the limit.

Ship life is as good or bad as you make it.

Don't be an ass and be respectful with your senior.
Ask questions to an experienced crewmember before deciding or signing your contract.

Don't work hard, work smart!

Save your money, be nice to everyone and trust NO one.

Make sure you logout off your internet!

Keep your business to yourself…the less they know about you the better.

First month is a hell. Learn fast the job and attend the trainings to have a better life later on. Don't expect to be welcomed with red carpet.

Stay hydrated!!

You embarked alone and you will disembark alone

If they can…you can! Work smart! Ship work never done!!!

Take a bottle of water on board the first day u arrive as u may not get your crew card until the next day and sometimes people are so busy rushing around they don't necessarily think "oh a newbie who might not know how to get the essentials!"

Go to crew bar. Even if you feel intimidated to start with. You will definitely get chatting to people and will learn how small the ship actually is. Everyone knows everyone.

Nothing good happens after 2am. Go back to your cabin.

The air con will dry u out soooo much. Take lip balm and drink lots of water.

If the ships clock changes in your first week you will be confused. Don't forget your phone will change itself.

Play safe. You never know…They always have a wife at home.

Go with the flow without forgetting the reason that made u choose ships.

Don't stress so much, don't take it so hard, be polite but don't allow anyone to take advantage of you, learn the rules and use them to your advantage

Follow rules, fight for yourself, first 3 months gonna be hell, later u get used to it. Switch off automatic time change on your phone, it may change at night and u get late for work. Work hard but have fun too. Its not all about money. Balkan ppl are just sounding rude, but get to know them u gonna fall in love.

Just try to do your best and play safe! Just make sure you know all well before you truly start a life onboard. Life is not truly easy working on a cruise ship as you are not on holidays. Sometimes hours may suck but you must try to work with your team. Teamwork helps a lot.

Focus and Succeed!

Don't drink with musicians or Russians—just joking, definitely do it! Hahaha.

Get ready for a new life-changing adventure. Welcome aboard!

CHAPTER 13

What Crazy Things PAX Do!

There is a list among cruise directors of crazy questions asked by passengers, commonly referred to as PAX. These have actually been asked, such as, "Where's the elevator to get to the front of the ship?" Or "Is the toilet water salt water or fresh…is it drinkable?" (What? Who cares?) And "Does the crew live onboard?" One passenger complained that she could no longer find her cabin because the ship had been parked backward!

Passengers are generally to be referred to as guests. The companies like to think that they have invited these folks into their ship as if they were invited into your own home (which it actually is since you live there!). However, guests do not always behave as guests. They are on vacation/holiday, and although there is a clear policy outlined for them regarding unacceptable language and behaviors, they don't always heed the rules. They may have bodily issues that are out of their control, take advantage of the extensive drink options to excess, or just generally behave badly! Despite the numerous sanitary facilities onboard, not all people seem to be able to find them when necessary. Following you will find some actual accounts of guest behaviors which may enlighten you about how a small percentage of the people might act onboard various ships.

The following stories are from many different cruise lines, numerous different crew positions, and offered for your amusement.

They have been left in the crew members' own words, with associated grammar and inflections.

> Once, this elderly female guest started doing very suggestive dance moves on a pillar. I'm serious, she was humping it and rubbing up and down against it. Very scary and hilarious at the same time.

> I was helping a VIP guest (65-ish of age) log on to the WiFi. His iPad was really dirty and I didn't want to touch it. I told him to go to Safari and go to the log-in website. Once he opened Safari there was sooooooooo much porn…all of it being young male teens. I pretended not to notice…

> A guy in his 50's was dressed as a baby (diaper, pacifier and a baby style hat) for the last 3 days of the cruise, because he lost a bet from his wife.

> A guest changed her clothes inside the photo gallery. And everybody saw this woman in underwear.

> We had a rather small group of rowdy 20-something year olds. They only lasted about 4 days (on a 10-day cruise) and were absolutely hammered 24/7. Shouting and hollering during all of the production shows. Numerous complaints from other passengers—including many of their hallway neighbors (surprise, surprise!) They ended up getting escorted off by security for skinny dipping in the pool during lunch time and getting belligerent with security and pool deck staff when asked to put on clothes…was not sad to see them leave!

WORK AT SEA, SEE THE WORLD: AN INSIDER'S SECRETS TO THE WORKING LIFE ON A CRUISE SHIP

I once saw a lady so drunk, dancing and stripping all around the guest service area—hahaha

Party of 7. Mom and Boyfriend, Dad and Girlfriend, 2 kids and nanny. They were celebrating their divorce and mom's new engagement the same night. 6 bottles of champagne later…mom and dad and new fiancé *very drunk* crying because the whole thing was a mistake and mom and dad were still in love. Eventually Dad and Fiancé slept in the dining room booth.

Well once I was working at a game table for the art gallery, and this older lady approaches me and I start doing my job, so I begin interacting and trying to make her guess the price of the artwork. She stares at me not speaking until I finish speaking, she then begins to get a bit closer, I back up because she is begging to invade my personal space, then again she steps closer and closer until she backs me up against the table. She then calls me David and tells me she was so happy to finally find me and tries to kiss me, I immediately move out of the way very freaked out. She looks me in the eyes again…Turns around and leaves! I report it to security. Turns out lady has 7 reports already! She had dementia and was going around trying to kiss everyone. Kinda sad really.

Guests crouching down to smoke marijuana at the back of the ship, right where our cruise staff office window was…called security regularly! 3-4 day cruises Bahamas.

A guest had to return a diamond ring worth $3000 to retail manager on the turnaround day as his credit card was declined. While his girlfriend was waiting for him (with their 2 year old baby) at the guest services to resolve the issue she informed me that "it was an engagement ring and her boyfriend had proposed her the night before…"

She was in tears and very embarrassed…

I watched, together with the assistant shop manager, a video that an old lady was stealing fake jewelry from the shops, shame on her!!

I was helping in the bottle shop and a young couple were in front being served. My teammate was scanning their items so I bent down to get a bag for their items when I loudly and very unexpectedly farted. He jumped out of the way and screamed like a big girl. I came up and was bright red. I couldn't look at the couple. Gave them their bag of items. They left the shop looked back at me where I was still embarrassed but laughing then as they were out of sight I heard the two of them burst into laughter! I never laughed so much in my life!

Me on the corridor, from one cabin a passenger storms out of his room and starts shouting to his wife that they will be late for their excursions because she wasn't ready yet, she was shouting from the room, he was from the corridor, big fight going on, all of the sudden he turns around saying that he's leaving and never coming back.

As Spa manager I had to deal with a guest taking pictures of women in the gym while they were bending over or stretching and a husband trying to beat the shit out of the guy!!

So this happened when I used to work at the pool (night shift). The pool is as dead as possible while I am cleaning, and this gorgeous lady walks up to me and says she is lost and she don't know how to reach her room. I did not realize she was tipsy. So, I start walking towards aft from fwd and she starts her sweet talks. She holds my hand saying I cannot balance, and well you seem like a gentleman, please hold my hand. I refrain as I don't wanna fall in trouble. She says then I'd like to sit otherwise I will fall in your arms. I so want that but then anyway…hahah. So she sits and starts flirting. I go and call security to escort her. I came back to her and she asks me if I am married. Although most men are bachelor's on ship and married outside back home, but me bachelor both sides. She tells me that she is married and then after 2 mins while I am waiting for security and scared at the same time. She said now that you know I am married, you are ignoring me and not wanna spend the night in my room with me. I was fucking jaw dropped. With a stone on my heart I had to ignore all the seductions. And control. Finally, security came I explained every bit and that she was going to be my hump for the night…haha.

Guests coming to perfume shop to fart…and then they even have the guts to use a perfume tester—yeah like a perfume can cover up your stinky ass.

Walking across pool deck to get to the buffet for dinner, old guy standing up in the Jacuzzi completely naked then "flossing" between his legs with a towel. Put me right off my dinner.

An old couple came to book their spa treatments, on their way out one of them farted and the wife said to the husband, is it you or is it me?

Every cruise story never ends. Guest leaving their personal details or asking are you on any social networking?—my reply: no ma'm sorry I can't afford ships Wifi.

Trying to look for the parents as one of the kids that is sick. Opened the photo of the parent on iPad to check the room number and the sibling of a sick kid goes: Oh, yes, yes…our poor mommy, looks so drunk…(speechless)

I remember while sitting at spa reception, a couple leaving the couples massage room with the furious wife at the front screaming and the two therapists following them. Apparently, the husband kept looking at the therapist and the wife got mad and made a scene.

A drunk guest peed herself in the middle of the promenade. Then she slipped in her own pee. She got up and then slipped again. Some people tried to help her get up, but no one wanted to touch her since she had pee all over.

Angry woman came to complain at the desk during high winds. Dress blew over her head and she couldn't get it down for ages!!! I was of course dying and wondering where to look…she didn't complain in the end.

Sex on the dance floor and orgy in the cabin, sex in the corner of corridor and gabbing the dick of the crew…that was 2014 on a Charter Cruise.

An elderly gentleman shat himself in the gym and walked straight past the toilets with diarrhea shit running down his trouser leg and dripping onto the carpet all the way to the elevators; it was spurting out and guests just stepping in all of it, not watching where they were going, spreading it everywhere. We had to shut down the corridor for two days; poor housekeeping staff had to clean it up—it smelt disgusting!

Well there's the multiple guests I've caught having sex in public.

There was the gay cruise. Watching hot guys everywhere naked, some banging and doing train choo choo choo…

I found a naked girl in the men's restroom. Completely drunk.

Passenger had dropped his binoculars over the side of the top deck and they landed behind the ship logo. Another passenger said, "Oh, I can get them" and started to climb over the railings on deck 14 whilst we were at sea. I managed to stop him and said I'd get a pool attendant to use a hook to pull them back over. He was completely oblivious to how dangerous climbing over the side of the ship was!

A husband was running with his daughter hiding from the wife, and he was carrying lots of balloons, he asked not to say where he was going, was so funny.

A guy peed on the planter box!!

A passenger in the photo gallery during my shift. They were watching firework footage on our TV. I left for a minute to say hi to one of the shoppies and on my return the pax was gone and in their place was quite a big pile of poo…Maybe the fireworks gave them a fright…

Having sex in the top deck pool we witnessed while setting up our buffet, then the wife or girlfriend caught them; a huge drama! That was my first contract.

A guest did a shit on stage during a dance class. Bingo had to be delayed

Dude shit in the mini-golf holes then took off his pants.

Somebody pooped in a plant.

Seeing this old skinny woman with sagging skin yet wearing a bikini with big boob implant.

Once, a beautiful woman I caught pissing on the drain on deck 4 toilet…she was so scared coz the automatic door opened and she was in that act. Apparently, she didn't know that she has to push the button to open the door to the toilet room! So she just pissed on the floor drain instead.

WORK AT SEA, SEE THE WORLD: AN INSIDER'S SECRETS TO THE WORKING LIFE ON A CRUISE SHIP

As a stateroom attendant on a charter cruise for swingers only, a couple of guests in my area had chiki chiki with the door open while I was doing the room that was in front of them.

Customer walking around the ship with tissue paper behind his shorts!!!!

One day I was on deck 13 from inside in the kitchen and it was morning 4:30 am and I saw one couple having sex on open deck openly—hahahhahah—that's the craziest thinks I saw ever.

Caught 3 teens hanging from the 11th deck railings doing pull ups...my heart almost stopped...after getting them up slowly I gave it to them!!

One papa did shit in the swimming pool and everyone disappeared from the pool within a second.

I was teaching a stretch class and this woman wore the wrong shorts (really wrong!) We were doing hamstring stretches on the floor and I look up to see what everyone is doing and I see pubic hair everywhere.

Overloading their plates at the buffet.

We had this pyramid scheme group that rented out the boat and they stole EVERYTHING. Would pick stuff up and just walk away and if you said hey, you need to pay for that they'd say they didn't know English and bolt. A sub group of them told my boss that I had offered the entire cruise free DVDs for the week (and my boss, being a complete moron, believed them and went off on me for an hour!)

Guests wear life jackets to crew drill.

Around 4 AM, a few teenagers were playing scavenger hunt naked and ran around the ship.

Mad guy jumped on top of the bar with a roll of toilet paper hanging from his shorts; he dances across the bar with the TP on fire. He was off the ship the next morning.

Did personal training with a naked passenger guy during the Bare Necessities Cruise

A drunk woman came to me crying and told me that she lost both of her lovers, they left her and she couldn't find them and if I could help her find her room on deck 12 because she doesn't know where it is. I escorted her to the nearest elevator.

In addition, here are some "complaints" that were collected, not from cruises, but from Thomas Cook Travel tour from 2015, as reported to Facebook by Peter Dickinson. They fit right into the crazy ways people behave and their expectations of their travels.
These are actual complaints:

They should not allow topless sunbathing on the beach. It was very distracting for my husband who just wanted to relax.

On my holiday to Goa in India, I was disgusted to find that almost every restaurant served curry. I don't like spicy food.

WORK AT SEA, SEE THE WORLD: AN INSIDER'S SECRETS TO THE WORKING LIFE ON A CRUISE SHIP

We went on holiday to Spain and had a problem with the taxi drivers as they were all Spanish.

We booked an excursion to a water park but no-one told us we had to bring our own swimsuits and towels. We assumed it would be included in the price.

The beach was too sandy. We had to clean everything when we returned to our room.

We found the sand was not like the sand in the brochure. Your brochure shows the sand as white but it was more yellow.

It's lazy of the local shopkeepers in Puerto Vallarta to close in the afternoons. I often needed to buy things during "siesta" time—this should be banned.

No one told us there would be fish in the water. The children were scared.

Although the brochure said that there was a fully equipped kitchen, there was no egg-slicer in the drawers.

I think it should be explained in the brochure that the local convenience store does not sell proper biscuits like custard creams or ginger nuts.

The roads were uneven and bumpy, so we could not read the local guide book during the bus ride to the resort. Because of this, we were unaware of many things that would have made our holiday more fun.

It took us nine hours to fly home from Jamaica to England. It took the Americans only three hours to get home. This seems unfair.

I compared the size of our one-bedroom suite to our friends' three-bedroom and ours was significantly smaller.

The brochure stated: "No hairdressers at the resort." We're trainee hairdressers and we think they knew and made us wait longer for service.

When we were in Spain, there were too many Spanish people there. The receptionist spoke Spanish, the food was Spanish. No one told us that there would be so many foreigners.

We had to line up outside to catch the boat and there was no air-conditioning.

It is your duty as a tour operator to advise us of noisy or unruly guests before we travel.

I was bitten by a mosquito. The brochure did not mention mosquitoes.

My fiancée and I requested twin-beds when we booked, but instead we were placed in a room with a king bed. We now hold you responsible and want to be re-reimbursed for the fact that I became pregnant. This would not have happened if you had put us in the room that we booked.

WORK AT SEA, SEE THE WORLD: AN INSIDER'S SECRETS TO THE WORKING LIFE ON A CRUISE SHIP

Special Cruises

Since we're talking about crazy guests, as you can see by the crew comments, there are often special groups that sometimes book the entire ship or host a group among the regular guests. Some of these groups are fairly innocuous and have special interests that keep them busy in the meeting rooms. There is a group coordinator assigned to fulfill any special request or needs they may have for equipment such as audio/video services, special power needs, etc. A small group may host a classic movie appreciation seminar, local history information, or religious study. A few groups host quilt-a-thons where about one hundred sewing machines are loaded onboard, and the electrical team has to coordinate with the stage staff to set up tables and chairs, unpack these machines, and run power to them all in a conference room. The guests that come for this group buy kits and supplies, and all these folks spend their sea days sewing up a storm!

And then there are the private groups who are a bit more hedonistic in their intentions. Usually the entire ship is chartered for these events. Swingers (who swap partners for sex), gay groups (male and female), drag groups and transgender groups, etc. Being on a ship provides them a place away from judgmental land authorities to indulge their desires and fantasies. They may have talent or fashion shows or special games. The pool decks may be set up with tents, or a dance lounge may be literally filled with mattresses, and all manner of crazy activities may take place that one would rarely see on land. But the crew, from all different countries, ethnicities, and religious backgrounds are suddenly thrust into the middle of this craziness and have to take care of the cleanup. Crew, of course, are never allowed to participate in these activities but will see things they may never have thought possible! The bands may sometimes be performing for a party of dancers that may be wearing little or nothing, and they can't let on that there is anything unusual about that! You may have some crazy stories to tell back home, for sure!

But you are living on the wide open ocean, and sometimes Mother Nature decides to join the party. She may throw you some surprises, so for those, you better be ready!

CHAPTER 14

What About the Weather?

The oceans deserve our utmost respect. They cover 70 percent of the earth's surface and have minds of their own, be it below the surface with currents and tides, or above it with fog, winds, and turbulence. At any time of year, there are a huge number of ships floating around the Bahamas, the Caribbean, the South Pacific, the South China Seas, the North Atlantic, the Baltic, the Adriatic, the Mediterranean, the Tasman, etc., and the likelihood of storms is ongoing and can pop up anywhere. Captains always do their best to avoid these as best they can. With all the sophisticated instruments on the bridge, they usually know where the hazards are and can adjust the itinerary to accommodate the weather changes. A port may have to be skipped or another substituted. The Caribbean has an annual hurricane season, so ships are on high alert from June 1 through November 30, with storm potential typically peaking in August, September, and October. But despite all the technological advancements, the sky and the ocean can both be unforgiving and unpredictable. Global warming has affected nearly all aspects of the weather. The old days of the big sailing ships being wrecked on reefs, or drawn under by giant waves is generally gone, and most danger can now be avoided with satellite information, extensive nautical charts, GPS, evasive maneuvers, and lots of power.

However, there may be times when there may be surf-size waves splashing out of the pool on the upper decks that force closures, as footing will be unsafe and slippery, not to mention the potential to be literally blown off your feet. Heed the safety warnings; they are there for your protection. Any outside worker, in any weather, will be required to don safety harnesses or proper protective equipment (PPE). You will learn about what to do in turbulent conditions, and preparedness alleviates most of the major concerns.

Storm Story

In September of 2017, I was on a ship in the Caribbean when Hurricane Mathew became a category 5 and hit Haiti, Cuba, the Virgin Islands, the Bahamas, and headed for Florida. We were in Cozumel, Mexico, at the time. The residents of Florida were advised to evacuate the coastlines. We were due back in Miami, but the port there was closed. So rather than heading into a storm (or even braving the tail of it) we sailed 187 miles southwest to Costa Maya, Mexico, and the guests enjoyed another beach day in the sun. With free Wi-Fi offered, there was lots of scrambling to alert family, petsitters, etc. about our whereabouts and to check on the safety of those at home and make flight changes. We got back three days late, but by then, all was well. The big movie screen in the theater showed news broadcasts to update us all on the storm track.

There may be periodic swells in the ocean that bring on the rock and roll. To avoid (or minimize) motion sickness, see chapter 15. In these circumstances, it is wise to wear flat shoes and use the handrails that are available nearly everywhere. Injury from falls (especially on a metal deck) are especially hazardous. Keep your balance or sit down, preferably somewhere where you can look outside toward the horizon. Whatever the situation, it will pass—maybe not right away but as soon as possible. The captains don't want *anybody* in danger or uncomfortable if they can possibly help it. Despite the stories (much like with airplane issues), the percentage of dangerous situations is very, very small compared to the huge numbers of ships in the oceans at any one time.

Crew Log

What were your scariest moments on a ship? (Some related to weather, some about general life onboard; in the words of the crew from a variety of cruise lines.)

> Once the seas were so ruff (back in 2011), and I decided to go out of the cabin and check the size of the waves, though when I went out I fall down three times and decided that it's time to go back and look for the life jacket PS: It lasted for 4–5 hours.

> Scariest and hilarious at the same time! A pipe line broke in the I-95 and water started to get in hallways and cabins nearby, I was taking a nap, and suddenly screams, people running and water running sound woke me up, opened the door water all over the hallway, still half asleep…I thought we were sinking!!!…scared the hell out of me…in my defense it was the first month of my first contract!

WORK AT SEA, SEE THE WORLD: AN INSIDER'S SECRETS TO THE WORKING LIFE ON A CRUISE SHIP

My husband (who was chief engineer at the time) had the most terrible experience…One of his engineers tried to make a run thru the water tight doors as they were closing (apparently it was something he had done a thousand times before) only this time he got stuck in the door as it closed. The rest you can only imagine…My husband still has nightmares about it…

35-40ft rogue wave hitting ship, severe listing. It was the day after Costa Concordia sank.

Being caught for days at sea in hurricane Lenny.

Sailing through the center of a hurricane in 2001.

An 11-hour fire in between Portugal and the Azores, for which we had nowhere near enough fire extinguishers, burnt most of our engines and sailed slowly to Madeira escorted by cargo ships.

At 5am…this is the bridge…we have been swiped by the wind and running into shore!

We rescued 150 Serian refugees, med staff helped them all night and in the morning they turned on us trying to hijack the ship. Thanks to many guys on our ship…they did not succeed, that's all I'm going to say.

Fire in the middle of the ocean and in the midst of hurricane Catherina after our ship had just finished the expansion.

Real "Bravo" onboard…When you heard on the PA system. This is not a drill…This is not a drill…Bravo…Bravo…Bravo…!!

Taken to the captain's office and ask about 50 random questions in which coast guards may ask should they come on the ship.

Abandon ship signal at 3am. Woke up, sat bolt upright in bed. The hallway was full of bleary eyed yet now VERY awake people. 2 mins later, an apology message from the bridge. I guess someone hit the wrong button?!

In February 2020, I was browsing Facebook and a passenger wrote a warning about 3 people testing positive for Covid 19 on our last cruise. I knew that lockdown was about to happen. Those first few weeks were so stressful that I would wake up in my isolated cabin at 4 in the morning absolutely terrified. Nothing was scarier than the beginning of the Corona virus outbreak. I eventually learned how to cope with the stress and got home.

Getting smashed by Hurricane Luis aboard in 1995…captain decided to outrun it, and left port straight for the storm.

When I thought I was pregnant!

Mine was a pastry Chef cut himself in his stomach and he almost bleed to dead.

Bravo bravo bravo in the middle of a formal night on deck 9 just beneath us!

Mine was 9/11 on a ship—we dock right in the heart of Manhattan.

When I was sent to photograph the body of a female passenger who had passed onboard. It was my first contract onboard in 2000.

Mine: DELAYED SALARY

Maitre'd office all the time hahahahah and u got mucho mistake u did and u dont know which one they knew

Huge storm off Bermuda. Everyone to remain in cabins. Waves washing over pool deck @level 14!

Cape Horn and last cruise of the South America season…worst experience and scariest.

I was the last person onboard in one of the Canary Islands. I arrived just as they were closing the door. Got a verbal warning for it.

Blackout while on our way to Ushuaia, for 30 mins.

When roomie walked in cabin while boyfriend messing with me from behind.

We had a hurricane that we sailed through twice, on the way to Mexico and back, then later on we had a fire in the elevator room so that was billowing smoke out onto the spa deck.

Hurricane Katrina.

Wake-up call from supervisor check in duty after 10 minutes late.

Late for the ship—NEVER AGAIN!

Unexpected wind blows our ship in 2018, we are in tender port, Montenegro. We nearly dock on the shore. I was in gangway for spa promotion, no damage or no injuries…we are blessed.

Ship when she listed a week after dry dock October 2018.

Was in ship from an we leave the port from Genova Italy to a port of Spain but in the middle of the sea we had a full blackout—only 1 engine was working as per the captain announce after 1 hour a tugboat come and we finally go to Marseilles port of France for 3 weeks for wetdock.

Kiss a guest in his room. And the knock the door like security, but was his auntie…Uffff. Never again!

But in storm or shine, should you find yourself in need of medical assistance, no worries! The medical team is on duty 24–7 and will handle whatever may arise. The next chapter will fill you in with more detail on how they take good care of you.

CHAPTER 15

Is There a Doctor in the House?

As you know, even before you were hired, you were sent a massive pile of medical forms that had to be completed by a doctor. The reason for the specific location directive was to ensure a measure of commonality and trustworthiness from authorized medical staff. The company needs to know if you have any pre-existing health issues, as once you are onboard, they take full responsibility for keeping you healthy. Any medications you take can usually be provided onboard (bring your prescriptions!), and if you find you have developed any illness, the medical staff onboard is there to help. Depending on the symptoms, you may be isolated to determine whether you are contagious or not. The medical facility onboard is very well equipped and professionally staffed. They take care of both guests (who are charged a fee) and crew (free, covered in your contract) and treat everything, from seasickness and stubbed toes to full-on respiratory issues, heart attacks, and broken bones. Whatever the diagnosis, your health is the most important priority, as well as keeping you from infecting anyone else. If other services are required, they're on it. I was in the port in Athens, Greece, when I lost a dental cap. The medical office arranged for a taxi to a dentist to fix it for me. I got an awesome round-trip taxi tour around town.

When the 2020 pandemic hit, everyone was required to be quarantined in their cabins, and procedures are still in place to protect (and feed) everyone by a special staff should any hazardous situation arise. The medical team is on alert for anything that may compromise the health and well-being of either crew or guests. They've been through it all and know how to handle even the most challenging situations.

Motion of the Ocean

If you are not accustomed to the motion of the ocean, the most common issue may be seasickness. Bear in mind that even if you feel queasy on small boats or winding roads, this may not affect you on a large ship. If it's any consolation, most of all astronauts take motion-sickness medication when in space. And no matter how conscientious your captain is in avoiding them, you may encounter occasional storms. There are treatments and meds available for this, no worries. Dramamine or Scopolamine patches may help. Check before you leave home that whatever you choose will not conflict with any other medications or opt for acupressure wristbands. If you are prone to these issues, take precautions ahead of time to be prepared. Bigger ships would be your best shot, as they are much more stable, and cabins located midship and on lower decks are the least prone to the effects of ocean motion.

Should you find yourself in a situation where the seas are full of large swells or storms, the best advice I can offer, as a lifelong sailor, is to stay somewhere onboard where you can see the horizon. Motion sickness has to do with your inner ear and your balance. If you can stay midships (as close to the middle) on a lower level outside deck, and can look out, it should help a lot. Drink plenty of water, avoid acidic foods (coffee, tea, orange juice, bacon, sausage) and instead eat bread, crackers, cereals, bananas, or green apples instead. Eating ginger and peppermint may help, or the smell of lavender (essential oils, potpourri, etc.). Try to stay standing or sitting upright when you can, as sometimes to lie down will make it worse. Avoid alcohol and cigarettes. And try not to focus on things that your brain normally thinks should not be moving: avoid reading a book, needlework, or looking through binoculars for extended periods. Breathe deep, hydrate, and look forward if you can rather than out a side window.

Crew cabins are typically on lower decks, but you'll luck out if you are located midship, and super bonus if you score an actual porthole or window. If you have an inside cabin, stay topside as long as you can. Personally the rocking side to side tends to put me right to sleep like that rocking of a baby's cradle.

Emergency Care

However, there may be medical situations that are beyond anyone's control onboard. In these cases, if the medical team deems it necessary, they will immediately transport you to the nearest port's hospital for more intensive care where there are more specialized physicians and more elaborate equipment. After treatment, once discharged from the need for medical care, you may be sent home or accommodated in a hotel for recuperation or further treatments until you are either cleared to return to duty or are sent home. If this is deemed necessary, your department head will be the one responsible for packing up your cabin, creating an inventory of your valuables, and sending your belongings to a port agent who will keep them safe until your release. This is very rare, but be assured, no matter what, you are always well taken care of!

Depending on the size of the ship and the company's requirements, there are generally two doctors, three nurses, equipment for an actual operating room, and several sick-bay spaces for patients. Several quarantine areas are available should someone need to be kept separate from others, most of which were expanded in 2020. In the return to service, most ships had dedicated sections of guest cabins allocated for this purpose to protect everyone. More info in chapter 23.

Packing checklist:

- ✓ Completed medical forms
- ✓ Passport
- ✓ Color photocopy of passport (kept separately for backup in case of loss)

- ✓ Medications for at least a month (and motion sickness if needed)
- ✓ Prescription copies (including eyewear if applicable)

A Rescue Story

While on a ship in the Caribbean, the sun had just peeked over the ocean's horizon, filling the sky with a hazy golden light at 6:00 a.m. on a waveless and calm morning. The lookouts on the bridge spotted a primitive raft floating aimlessly in the misty dawn, and our rescue boat was dispatched to investigate. Shortly thereafter, a tender boat was sent out to pick up seventeen people that had been trying to "sail" from Cuba to Miami on a crude barrel-type raft with nothing but a torn bedsheet as a sail. The people we rescued were malnourished, having run out of food, and were sunburned and dehydrated. Their paltry belongings were stuffed into big black trash bags as they abandoned their meager craft and were brought onboard. These bedraggled survivors were isolated in one of the conference rooms which was outfitted with mattresses and blankets. Those in the worst condition were taken to the medical facility for treatment. We were on our way to Cozumel, Mexico, and upon arrival, they were disembarked first, each in a wheelchair. Three were on gurneys and transported to the hospital, the others loaded into a van. Each of them was attired in new company T-shirts, shorts, and flip-flops. I had to smile at the one lady who had bleached blond hair and long red fingernails. She was apparently preparing to blend in with the fashionistas in Miami! I had to wonder how she had survived without breaking a nail! Cuban law dictates that anyone picked up at sea must be repatriated back to Cuba. I don't know whatever happened to that courageous bunch of drifters. Standing at the rail, we watched them taken away and sent prayers for their recovery and safety, hoping that someday they might find their freedom.

All in all, despite the stories, it has to be emphasized that the chances of this being a life-threatening job are very, very low; for the hundreds of thousands of crew members in the industry, a minute percentage find that there are any health or injury issues. Sanitizing is done constantly, and cleanliness is paramount. As for any accidents, each ship tracks the numbers of accident-free days proudly, and every effort is made to ensure everyone's safety. Proper protective equipment (PPE) is always provided for the appropriate job. Each crew member is asked monthly to submit ideas in a safety report to prevent any foreseeable issues; if you see something, say something. But hey, there are thousands of traffic accidents that threaten lives every day, and we don't stop driving! Just sayin'.

So you're safe onboard, but what about going ashore? Everybody asks about the ports. Yes! Go! They are amazing and will create so many experiences and memories for you from all parts of the world. Coming up, you will get some info that will help you enjoy these experiences to the max!

CHAPTER 16

Can You Get Off in the Ports?

This is the number 1 question I am asked about life on a ship: "Can you get off in the ports?" Well, the short answer is yes, and no. Under normal circumstances, that is the magic of this job. You may go to places you may have never heard of or never dreamed of visiting. Many places you may visit repeatedly and may come to know as well as you do your own hometown (or better!). However, the events of 2020 put a serious kink in this plan. As cruising tried to recover from the global pandemic, not only were the ships halted from sailing, but many of the countries closed their ports also. Every country was wary of foreigners, and the skeleton crews that continued to keep the ships operational were not allowed shore leave. Supplies were delivered, but no one could go out. This took its toll on crew morale, but as the ships started to return to service, extensive protocols were instituted for ultimate safety. New sign-ons were quarantined for two weeks, everyone endured daily temperature checks, and biweekly PCR tests were instituted for all crew. Guests could not sail without a negative test prior to boarding and were checked upon debarkation to confirm negative results.

Shore leave was cancelled until the situation was under control, but that did not deter crew who were anxious to return to work and get back to sailing. Morale took a hit, but crew members were tolerant and understanding of the situation. The safety of everyone was paramount, and for a while, the visits to the ports could wait.

WORK AT SEA, SEE THE WORLD: AN INSIDER'S SECRETS TO THE WORKING LIFE ON A CRUISE SHIP

Actually the safety bubble onboard was the best place to be! As normality returns to the industry, consider these criteria when in anticipation of your adventures in ports for each location of your itinerary:

1. Topography
2. Temperatures
3. Cultural requirements
4. Activities
5. Excursions
6. Languages

The adventure begins! Regardless of where your first contract takes you, I hope you will be excited at the prospect of exploring some place new. Besides the challenge of finding your way around the ship, settling into crew life, and getting to know your fellow crew members, the lure of foreign ports is irresistible. Once you know your itinerary, look at a world map to get a visual on exactly where you are headed! Research some information on the culture and be aware if there are any religious accommodations to consider. Get familiar with the important landmarks, the must-see locations, the history, major events, and the weather. It will help you pack to know if you might need a headscarf to visit a mosque, water shoes for climbing a waterfall, boots for mountain hiking, or a hat and warm coat.

Typically, wherever the ship is going, most often (but not always) it docks early in the morning. If your schedule allows, some ports are worth getting your butt out of bed to watch the dawn sail in. Don't miss the morning light bathing the canals of Venice, the dawn glowing off the Sydney Opera House, the magnificent luminescence of the Alaskan glaciers at daybreak, or the spectacle of the dramatic New Zealand waterfalls. The birth of a new day casts a uniquely anticipatory glow over these famous landmarks and is not to be missed.

Once docked, it will take time for the ship to be cleared by the local authorities, and you may need to wait to disembark until after the gaggles of guests have finished crowding the gangways. The gangway location could be on the portside this week and the starboard side the next time, even if you have returned to the same place. It can also vary with the tides, and the deck location may change. The crew usually disembarks on a lower deck accessible from the I-95 via their own gangway, separate from the guests. Crew are restricted from taking certain items on or off the ship, and you may be required to reveal the contents of your backpack. Food is never to be taken off, especially in some ports where there are stringent restrictions regarding potential infestations. Some ports even have dogs (Mexico, Spain, New Zealand, etc.) that will sniff everyone's belongings to ensure compliance, and there can be stiff fines for "smuggling" an apple.

There are two ways you may disembark. Usually it's a simple matter of walking off the gangway to find it's a few steps to the middle of town. In other places, you may dock in a cargo port where a shuttle bus will take you off the pier. Once outside the port area, you will nearly always have to negotiate a maze of souvenir shops before finding either a town or a path to get there. It may be walkable, or it may require a taxi or a bus, depending on how far the port is from the city center. Sometimes a bus is gratis; other times there may be a small fee, but usually a crew discount is available with your ID. Remember the requirement for comfortable walking shoes? Make mental note of time and landmarks to make your way safely back (and in plenty of time!).

The second method of debarkation is by tender boat. When there is no dock for the ship, or the waters are too shallow, it is necessary to anchor offshore. Sometimes the locals will have large tour boats that carry several hundred people; other times you will be taking one of the modified lifeboats, called a tender, to be shuttled. The guests get first dibs, so be patient and wait your turn. There will be a lineup, so be sure you have taken everything you need with you, as it's tough to go back for anything once you've gotten into the queue. Photo ID, sunglasses, camera, sunblock, phone, umbrella, money, and the laptop if you are off in search of extended Wi-Fi time.

If there are fee-based activities in the port, such as an animal sanctuary, botanical garden, or museum, be sure to ask if there are crew discounts, and show your ID. Or enjoy your day at the beach, your tour of ancient forts, lunch of local cuisine (check before you go inside that they have Wi-Fi), or a shopping trip for souvenirs or snacks. *Always* keep an eye on the clock, and be aware of whether you are expected to stay on *ship* time or *local* time (more often the former). Allow enough transport time to get back before you are required to be. Don't rely on your phone time! Wearing an analogue watch is advisable. Take special note of your path: How did I get here? How long did it take? And what's the way back? I once walked for miles and then had to backtrack in the heat of the blazing Casablanca sun before I realized there was only one road across the fenced railroad tracks!

To return to the ship from either a dock or a tender pier, you will often go through two ports of inspection where everything goes through the x-ray. The shore terminal may have one for the country, and the ship yet another. Crew will have their own queues, and again, the only food that may come back onboard is what is packaged; no leftovers from lunch, no awesome French pastries. Any fresh food like fruits, vegetables, or meat, even packaged, is usually not allowed. Crew are also expected to remove their shoes and may be patted down by security; slip-on shoes are always an advantage to keep the line moving. Flip-flops are allowed, but only for getting on or off the ship.

Sydney Opera House

Generally the ships spend the majority of their time in ports with lots of sun, beaches, and shopping. Europe provides more historical options, but again, lots of walking in the summer heat, be it Naples, Rome, or Athens. Be prepared with good walking shoes, a sun hat, and sunscreen. The only exceptions to the beach habit are the ports in Alaska (where it can still be 80 degrees) and the Baltic (Scandinavia, Russia, etc.) or anything northward, such as Canada or Newfoundland, where layers are always advised so you can bundle up if need be. Frankly I found it to be colder in New Zealand than it was in Alaska! But honestly, if there is anything you find you think you should have brought, it can be purchased at just about any of your destinations. And when buying it there, you are supporting the local economy, and you have an awesome (and useful) souvenir of your travels.

Port Adventures

One of the joys I found of ship life as a crew member was the opportunity to accompany guests (for free!) on the guest excursions. Not all ships or all lines allow this, but ask. At the start of each cruise, there was a sign-up notebook near the excursion office for crew. I reviewed the excursion options from the guest brochures to choose my preferences. Then first come, first served at the sign-up binder. If there are some extremely popular tours (like the Parthenon in Athens), there are usually several busses assigned, so the chances of getting an excursion are good. As an escort, I was the liaison between the ship and the company who provided the guides. I filled out a report on the names of the guide and bus driver, noted times out and back, and took note of how well the guide spoke English, if they used amplification (and how well it worked), and how I assisted should there be any incidents. For example, in climbing a castle in Malaga, Spain, a guest tripped on the uneven pavement and took a header onto the bricks. The guide had to continue with the rest of the group, so I tended the lady's minor cuts and stayed with her until the group came back. The guide brought her some wine, and that seemed to make everything better! An escort is a support to the guests and provides valuable feedback to help the shore excursion team improve the experiences. I kept a log of my excursions with details and notes on how much the guests had paid for these adventures. I figure I have taken more than seventy-four tours and had mountains of fun. I can't count how many times I've climbed the hill to the Parthenon! Guests are fascinated by the crew experience and will ask lots of question. Be diplomatic, positive, and a bit vague with your answers as frankly, the secrets of crew life are best remaining secret for the general public. (Shh...remember, these are secrets!)

As an alternative, if your schedule allows, some lines will allow you to pay for the guest excursion and give you a crew discount. Enjoy the ride and relish the opportunity! Take a paperback travel guide or download some online info for your ports so you can maximize your time ashore and be ready to see what interests you beyond the typical tourist bits. The website *www.RickSteves.com* has self-guided audio tracks of walking tours you can download to your phone, and lots of invaluable previsit information for numerous parts of the world.

Language

Communicating in the various languages of the world can sometimes be a challenge. Not everyone (obviously) speaks English nor should we expect them to. Although it is required onboard for maritime safety, in a foreign country, be open to basic communication skills in the country's language. Many places have folks who do speak English (look for the younger generation; it's often mandatory in schools), but I have found it helpful to learn at least these phrases in whatever language I might expect to encounter:

1. Hello
2. Goodbye
3. Please
4. Thank you
5. Pardon me
6. Can you write it down please? (Good for numbers, addresses, things you don't understand, etc.)

7. And an extra bonus, "Excuse me, where is the toilet?" (The *bathroom* or *restroom* are American terms that more literally equate to where you want to take a bath or need to wait.)
8. You could learn "how much," but the answer may leave you bewildered.

Granted there are apps that can translate phrases or provide crucial words, but those essential phrases are basic courtesy. There are also portable translators, but I have yet to find one that actually works well without sucking up data, requiring Wi-Fi access, or the study of lengthy tutorials on the "easy" operation. I've taken careful (and phonetic) notes from tour guides and taxi drivers who are usually so excited to find people interested in communication and are more than willing to share their knowledge. In a pinch, the *Google Translate* app can be a lifesaver, at least in restaurants that have Wi-Fi.

Nothing beats personal language lessons, but to try on your own, *Babble* or *DuoLingo* apps are helpful. My personal favorite is a downloadable audible program available at *Pimsleur.com* for access to over fifty-one languages. (See https://buyersguide.org/language-learning-software for comparison shopping and rates.) Some programs have free introductory lessons, are very inexpensive for more lessons, and are completely auditory. If you have a good ear, it's easy to pick up what you need. Having used several of these programs, I found it amusing that they use the same script for each, such that it usually starts with a scenario of "an American man meets a 'fill in the blank' woman." The interactions can be amusing, and I now know if I'm being picked up in several languages. After listening to these programs in French, Spanish, and Portuguese, when I heard this in Mandarin, I had to laugh yet again. At one point, the man always asks, as they arrange to meet for dinner, "Shall I meet you at the restaurant or pick you up at the hotel?" The answer she gives is, "I'll meet you at the restaurant." To which he always replies, "Okay, I'll see you at the hotel." Seems that men always want to hear what they prefer (sorry, guys).

Your ship may provide access to a language lab onboard where you can learn a multitude of languages with *Rosetta Stone*, a program that would cost you hundreds of dollars on your own. Here, it's free! When you have time to sit and study and see the words, it will reinforce your skills. It's also available if you need to polish your English a bit. Another option for those moments of free time.

Currency

Most of your purchases for sundries, like laundry detergent, toothpaste, or deodorant, can be purchased onboard in the slop chest. However, the object is to experience the local fare for which the local currency is often required to support a merchant or grab a coffee. You can purchase most things with a credit card if you prefer, just be sure to get one that does *not* have foreign transaction fees, as these will add up quickly. For local currency that you'll need in farmer's or artisan's markets, you can get money changed onboard in the financial office. Sometimes there are conversion kiosks or ATMs in the port terminal. If I know I will be in a particular country often, I sometimes get more of that currency, either before I leave home through my bank or change some money at the arriving airport, usually through an appropriate ATM. Try not to convert more than you will need, but don't get caught short either. Conversion back to your home currency will usually incur an additional charge, and coinage can't be converted, only paper money. Use up those coins in the airport vending machine or donate them in the bins offered for charity before leaving the country. Traveling in Europe is great where so many counties use the Euro. You can travel between France, Spain, and Italy and no longer have to worry about Francs, Pesetas, or Lire. That multipocket wallet or change purse will come in handy to separate the coinage for other country's currencies.

Put a currency exchange app on your phone to help calculate what exactly you are spending. I use one called *XE*. Knowing the equivalent to your own currency will help immensely until you get used to the money. In some countries like Spain, Mexico, or Turkey, the merchants expect you to bargain, so be sure to investigate the cultural norms beforehand for your destinations. Carry small bills and coins for the best bargaining. Also find out if restaurants automatically tack on a service fee or if you need to add a tip. You don't want to double up, but you also don't want to offend. In France, it's customary to round up your tab to leave some extra (if your bill is 18 euros, leave 2 more on the table). Be prepared ahead of time with some advance research or ask a local. Don't rely on the advice of the waiter!

Wi-Fi

Often the primary reason to go ashore is to find some extensive Internet access, enjoy some local cuisine, or go to a Seafarers' Center. A daily schedule should have port-agent information in case of emergency. In port, beware of getting so caught up in your online experience that it's easy to lose track of time! Keep an eye on your belongings, and don't hang a purse or backpack behind you on the back of a chair; keep things in view! Set an alarm on your phone or watch to alert you to allow you to log off, pack up, and get back to the ship by "all aboard" time, usually an hour ahead of the guests. Allow for weather, walking, or shuttle busses. Every time you leave or enter the ship, your identity card is swiped in the electronic scanner, and the ship knows exactly who has left and when (or if!) they have come back. If, for some crazy reason, you don't come back to the ship, they would know it, but they very well may leave without you! Another reason to go out with a friend. You do not have possession of your passport (it is being held by HR) so being left in a foreign country creates a myriad of complications. *Don't let it happen!* If you get left behind, security is alerted, and this sets a whole series of procedures in motion, but suffice it to say, you're in serious trouble! Remember, there are extensive repercussions for "jumping ship." If there is an emergency, take note of the port agent's contact info, usually noted on the shopping or port information sheets that are available before you leave the ship. Contact them immediately.

WORK AT SEA, SEE THE WORLD: AN INSIDER'S SECRETS TO THE WORKING LIFE ON A CRUISE SHIP

Port Manning

You may not be able to go out at all. Defined and explained in chapter 10 with trainings.

When in Rome

As an American, I have become aware that other countries may have varying opinions of my country. If you are from elsewhere, skip this part, but I offer it up for the awareness of my fellow citizens. Others may see us as the "land of the free and the home of the brave," but when we travel, we seem to feel we can take our country (and our customs and behaviors) with us rather than attempting to fit into our new surroundings. So FYI, I offer this report from Europeans who can pick us out from a crowd (before we open our mouths with our distinctive American accents).

These are tips to identify Americans who typically

1. request ice in their drinks;
2. wear baseball caps (frontward or backward);
3. wear white socks with sandals (really, guys?);
4. may have perfect extra-white teeth;
5. often are not aware of different customs (Brits dip their fries in mayo, not ketchup);
6. call you bro;
7. sport strange attire: wear gym shoes (or trainers) with shorts and fanny packs; maybe an adult with kid's accessories (a Spider-Man backpack?);
8. don't recognize that football is actually soccer to the rest of the world;
9. eating while walking, or doing anything else (eating is for the joy of it);
10. don't understand Celsius or meters (learn conversions!);
11. are bewildered by the obsession with McDonald's;
12. don't recognize alcoholic limits (never drinks to-go, what is the rush?);

13. are prudish about nudity;
14. talk too loudly, especially around strangers or other Americans;
15. need to learn some of the local language; just talking loudly will not clarify the intention;
16. are confused about tipping (research before hitting a restaurant or hailing a taxi);
17. should learn when it is (or is not) appropriate to haggle or bargain;
18. shouldn't try to adopt (badly) the local accent;
19. haven't researched customs, manners, and especially gestures;
20. often wear graphic T-shirts with verbiage, or wear North Face gear;
21. typically carry way too much luggage;
22. take too many selfies and always have eyes on their phones;
23. are often overweight (thanks to McDonalds and KFC);
24. should use headphones, not a boombox;
25. should never, never litter!

My fellow Americans, please research your destination or attach yourself to a local to learn the customs and integration techniques. The world is full of amazing people and places. *Respect* is the magic word! Learn a bit of the language and behave yourself, please. The world will keep on turning, even without you back home keeping an eye on things. Adopting this life may require some changes in perspective. Broadened horizons will expand your ways of thinking, so just be aware—look out, you are growing! Wow.

CHAPTER 17

Life Flows on Within You and Without You...

In the immortal words of Beatle George Harrison, "Life flows on within you and without you." You will be away from home for months on end, and life back home will indeed carry on without you. Yes, believe it or not, they will survive—somehow! You will find ways to stay in touch by e-mail, FaceTime, Skype, Zoom, or whatever the current technology will allow. But kids will grow up, birthday parties will happen, there may be weddings, graduations, births, and even deaths and funerals that will not be a part of your life during those months. But take heart, actual emergencies can be accommodated if absolutely necessary. If Grandma is on her last legs, it will take some quick HR maneuvers, but they will try to get you home to bid her a fond farewell. It might cost you some coin for personal expenses, but HR may be able to do some quick finagling to cover your absence, and hopefully it will be short-term, and Grandma will be back on her feet in no time.

Story

The drummer in the Filipino party band needed to go home from the Caribbean as his father was very ill. He petitioned for a leave of absence for a two-week period. So the drummer from the jazz trio offered to cover for him. The songs were widely known standard rock fare, but this meant having to play two lounges in sets back-to-back and made for a *very* long night and very tired limbs several nights in a row! If you know that you have family or other obligations, earliest possible notice is the best advice. Other departments' heads are typically very understanding of circumstances and will help as best they can. But you are the only one doing your particular job.

It will be hard to feel completely separate from your home life, but once you get into the groove of your life onboard, your attention will be refocused. There will be work time, sleep time, free time, and connection time, where you can get caught up on what's happening at home. It may be tough to maneuver around time zone differences, and a challenge to find the optimum crew-area spot with adequate connection availability (you are in a big metal box moving on the ocean), but you will find a way. Technology makes it all possible, so be sure your cell phone plan or other electronics will accommodate your location communication needs to facilitate face-to-face or voice contact.

You may find there are things you will miss from home: the independence of driving a car, the sound of absolute silence, walking on a floor that doesn't move, the sound of morning birds, the sight of trees outside your window—or even having a window for that matter! You will be living in one room (perhaps half a room if you are sharing), and your sense of time in the day, days in the week, and weeks in the month will blend into one another to where you actually have no clue as to where you are or what day it is! Beware of relying too heavily on your cell phone clock too. There may be time changes that will throw you completely out of kilter and mess with your head! Keep an eye on the ship info channel on your cabin TV. That analogue clock I suggested will come in handy, as it's easy to change as you move around the globe. And sometimes the changes are weird, like a half hour forward tonight, then an hour forward tomorrow, then turning them back again—*what?* Telling time can be crazy in various parts of the world.

The opportunity for excursions in port will help keep you in touch with the earth, and there may be opportunities to get out of your floating metal box and away from the cargo port and souvenir shops to experience some nature in a park or a garden like the Tasmanian Botanical Garden in Hobart, Acadia National Park in Maine, or Dunn's River Falls in Jamaica. Take advantage of the chance to walk in grass, sit beneath trees, smell flowers, enjoy the majesty of waterfalls. But those excursions may be short-lived as you watch the clock anxiously (What time is it *here*? I am supposed to stay on ship time, right?) before you head back to that giant metal floating box, take heart, you might be back here again next week!

You may find that time seems to stand still. Your routine will blend one day into the next, and before you know it, you will be packing your gear to go home. I find that there is a sadness to signing off. Your crewmates have been your new family for many months, and frankly, there is no guarantee you will see them again. Everyone lives on a different contract time frame. Collect personal contact information for those that are important to you so you can stay in touch. There are also online groups that help you connect (e-mail, Facebook, Instagram, Snapchat, etc.), but enjoy the time you have together. The ship experience, even if you come back to the same ship, will not be the same. Relish the time you have together and the unique excitement of your first contract adventure.

Congratulations! You made it!

And not all days will be the same routine. You may find your ship is not headed for the beaches this week after all, but off to a maintenance appointment with a dry dock. That's a whole different kettle of fish. Yep, even more new adventures await!

CHAPTER 18

What is Dry Dock?

Generally every five years, each ship is sent to a shipyard for refurbishing and maintenance. This is sometimes referred to as a revit, for revitalization. Under normal circumstances, as the ship sails, there is a constant running inventory by those in charge regarding the condition of every part of the ship, from the top of the antenna mast to the bottom of the keel. Everything in between, such as the engines, the propulsion systems (propellers, Azipods, bow thrusters, etc.), the processing machinery for waste and fresh water, condition of upholstery and furniture, the electronic and electrical systems, and everything else is noted on a daily basis by carpenters, electricians, and engineers.

For anything in need of service, there are three ways these repairs can be accomplished:

1. As the ship has repair shops onboard for machinery, carpentry, plumbing, upholstery, etc., the small repairs can be done in the course of regular service. Broken barstools, torn upholstery, etc. are just a very small part of the overall daily maintenance. The busiest guys are often the plumbers who are called upon to respond to a TNF (a toilet not flushing). The central facilities office manages the dispatch of repair persons to address any correctable situation. Machinery and electronics are all tended to as quickly as possible.

2. Second, for more major maintenance or repair issues, is the process of wet dock. For this the ship sails into a shipyard somewhere in the world that can accommodate its size. With no guests onboard, the ship may remain afloat and moored in the shipyard while contractors come onboard to accomplish the necessary repairs. The gangway may be primitive with metal mesh or wooden plank walkways and a flimsy handrail. As the ship is moored, it is subject to the tides, and certain times of the day make the gangway trek literally an uphill battle. Some external hull repairs can be accomplished by divers, but most often, wet dock is used to complete interior changes like converting a lounge area into a specialty restaurant, adding slides and fun stuff to the pool deck, interior remodeling, electrical work, updating the Internet electronics, or other such adjustments that cannot easily be accomplished with guests aboard.

3. Third is the ultimate haul out into dry dock. Again off to a large shipyard where the ship is carefully maneuvered into a concrete and metal channel. A giant metal door closes behind the ship, and all the water is drained out, and the keel comes to rest on preset large concrete blocks. Since the ship is literally high and dry, the access to the gangways can be a major challenge. This is accomplished by hiking up *lots* of switchback stairs. Beware that if you have to board here, hauling luggage up this labyrinth will be a challenge to both muscles and patience. Then there is an obstacle course of equipment, cranes, lines and tools to maneuver to get to the gangway access. If you are onboard and want to go out, that decision will include whether you want to brave this obstacle course or not, and whether, if you plan to return late after a drink or two after dark, you can actually manage this safely. Your daily job may be adjusted to support maintenance crews, so you have to be flexible and accommodating to meet the repair schedule.

Over 150 metal stairs plus an obstacle course
for access…don't try it in the dark!

Putting the ship into dry dock is essential for access to the propellers, stabilizers, and bottom fixtures. Some ships have Azipods.

WORK AT SEA, SEE THE WORLD: AN INSIDER'S SECRETS TO THE WORKING LIFE ON A CRUISE SHIP

Developed in Finland, an Azipod is a marine propulsion unit consisting of a fixed pitch propeller mounted on a steerable gondola, which also contains the electric motor driving the propeller. These are amazing inventions as the entire assembly can rotate 180 degrees such that the ship can literally turn on a dime and sail sideways! They are each controlled separately from the bridge or the engine control room and make maneuvering a piece of cake. Rarely is an Azipod-equipped ship in need of a tugboat. But when they need service, a dry dock is necessary for complete access for repair or possible replacement.

Azipods on display

The keel blocks

A shipyard is not a pretty place, even if it may sound like an exotic location like the Bahamas, France, or Spain; it all depends on where the dock is actually situated. Security gates are tight, and authorized identification is required. It's usually a very basic facility with massive paved or gravel areas where large containers of supplies are parked to be loaded onboard by huge cranes. There may be minimal amenities in the immediate vicinity for off-duty diversions. Sometimes there are local shuttle busses provided to take you to a market, nearby restaurant, or some local shopping, but they may run on particular schedules, and heaven help you if you miss the last one to get back onboard. If these are not offered, and the location is not near the town, taxis can get expensive. Although the gangway is generally open 24–7 while work is in progress, there are some locations where you really don't want to be out at night and certainly never alone.

While docked in a shipyard, all the interior surfaces are covered for protection: plastic is laid on all the flooring, rough plywood panels are inserted into the elevators to protect the walls from damage as equipment and personnel move supplies and tools around. All furniture is covered, as is wall art and anything else deemed vulnerable. Obviously there are no guests onboard but lots of men in coveralls and tool belts everywhere from all manner of various countries. The various contractors accommodated in the guest cabins are in charge of electrical work, engine machinery, interior decor, carpeting, etc. Both crew and guest cabins may even be accessed for repairs and refurb when necessary, and occupants may be moved temporarily. This time may also be used to change over theater show casts from one contract to another. These performers may be onboard from six to nine months for a contract, so dry dock is an opportune time to board the new cast for rehearsals, costume fittings, and orchestra prep while there are no guests expecting to be entertained.

WORK AT SEA, SEE THE WORLD: AN INSIDER'S SECRETS TO THE WORKING LIFE ON A CRUISE SHIP

Dining in Dry Dock

Sometimes the guest and crew buffet areas are under repair, so food service may be provided in the main dining room, but it's not the sit-down-and-get-served style as in a normal cruise—you are not a guest! The chairs are covered in giant black trash bags to protect the upholstery from workers' dirty coveralls, and the tables covered in plastic. The big buffet in the center of the room will all be self-serve, and often the use of the ship's water is limited for repairs, so rather than wash dishes, food is served on paper plates and eaten with plastic utensils. The culinary selections are fairly limited, but there is some variety. There is always lots of rice!

There are times when they decide to flush the water system, and there is no water available for hours on end. This means no showers, and use of the toilet is fine, but no flushing! *Ew!* This also means no ice for food or drinks for possibly many days. When the water is again restored to operation, it goes through a series of chemicalization processes where there is a large amount put into the system for it to flush through, and you still can't use it for hours (or days).

Once the testing team from each deck reports to the control center regarding the parts per million (ppm) level, the use can't be restored until levels are balanced and back to normal. This may be the time you want to go out to a local restaurant, not only for culinary variety but also for the use of the bathrooms!

They may turn off the power without warning, so unplug your electronics to avoid surges upon resuming operation. You may need to move if there is work in your cabin area or be subjected to constant noise (drilling, hammering, etc.) that may not allow you much sleep. The contractors work at all hours, every day and night, as maintaining the timeline is crucial to the operation. The air-conditioning may be shut off for a while, and it may get unbearably hot. A small battery-operated fan could be a godsend. You are still expected to complete your daily Kronos (the computerized recording system) for your work times, and you must finish whatever jobs you have been assigned.

The Disposal System

Some people have a mistaken impression that cruise ships are responsible for the massive waste accumulating in the oceans. I can assure you this is far from the case! The oceans are the support system for the industry, and cruise ships are dedicated to respecting the environment, not contributors to the pollution. Many people are often curious about the water and trash systems onboard. I'm not an engineer (hell, I'm a musician!), but I can tell you that the water and waste systems are extremely efficient and exceptionally eco-responsible. I can't speak for all the companies, but the ones for which I have worked go above and beyond the mandatory regulation levels for clean in the processing of whatever waste is expelled into the ocean and never near land.

The gray water and black water (sewage, machine oil, etc.) are all fed through a bio-something system that literally has microorganisms that love to eat this stuff, and in turn they change the composition into what they can certify as clear and "drinkable"—even though of course, nobody would. It is, however, used to water the plants onboard. The largest ships have an actual Central Park with hundreds of thousands of plants to water; everything is recycled.

Food waste (and granted there is quite a lot) is all processed through a similar system that dilutes and grinds it down to minute particles to the cleanest levels possible before it is expelled into the ocean in the widest open spaces (never closer than twelve miles offshore of any landmass), and the fish get well fed. All part of the food chain! Nothing pollutant or toxic, all decomposable.

All trash is sorted, and combustibles are incinerated, but again, even if you see smoke from the funnels on top of the ship, they are also treated to screen out pollutant waste, and what you see is generally harmless steam or "clean" smoke. The cruise industry is well aware that they rely completely on the safe and clean use of the oceans for their longevity. It serves no one to harm any part of the environment, and tremendous research and engineering expertise has been exerted to create the safest and cleanest ways to process all the products that come on board. Currently many fuel systems are being converted from diesel to natural gas and other clean propulsion materials. There are even oceanographic testing systems installed on some ships that report constantly to organizations monitoring and assessing climatic changes, so they are actively contributing to the observation and recording of vital atmospheric conditions.

Any nonprocessable waste, such as glass, metal, cardboard, etc., is all recycled. All trash is carefully separated and treated. Glass is separated by color, crushed, and barreled. Metal is flattened and bundled. Cardboard is flattened and strapped in bales. Medical waste is transferred to responsible businesses ashore. These materials are all off-loaded in various ports on turnaround day where they are turned over to reputable recycling companies.

Hopefully you will have the opportunity to get a tour of some of these processes. You will learn about them in training, and you will get a chance to visit the bridge to see the operational systems, the fire alarm systems, the navigational systems, etc. The galleys, food lockers, and refrigerators are fascinating to see. Everybody wants to see the liquor locker! There is a process for everything, including which crates of bananas are stored in front versus in back for efficient use according to ripeness, etc. The massive main laundry cleans literally mountains of sheets and towels every day, and options for minimal changeover for both are always offered and encouraged in support of the Save the Waves movement. A ship is an intricate spiderweb of processes that provide everything people need and is operated on an amazingly efficient system to keep everyone healthy and well fed while still protecting the environment. Literally, a floating city! Please join the efforts to support the longevity of the clean-ocean efforts by purchasing products at http://www.4Ocean.com or contributing to https://www.OceanConservancy.org. Thank you.

CHAPTER 19

How Do You Get Outa Here?

Well, you are free to leave anytime. But if you decide to break contract, you have to cover your own expenses to do so and can just about kiss the chance of another contract goodbye. You throw everyone into a panic to replace you on short notice. So if you've stuck it out, this contract has been somewhere between four, six, nine months or more. Daily routine can become redundant and tedious, yet free time can be a blast. The friends you make onboard can be lifelong and international in nature. You may find yourself visiting the Ukraine or Norway someday as a result of onboard friendships. Be sure to collect e-mails, phone numbers, and utilize social media to stay in touch. Returning to your hometown can seem like a backward step. You may find it's impossible not to chime in on a conversation with, "When I was in Venice…" or "I remember one time in Bora Bora…" While thrilling to you, it may put others off who are stuck in Podunk, Somewhereland, and may never travel beyond the county line. Resist the temptation to name-drop. If they ask about your travels, tell them your stories; otherwise it might be well to hold that thought.

But as they say, all good things must come to an end. For me, I love new beginnings. It's kind of like that first day of school when it's all ahead of you, and you're not behind in your homework—yet. But you cannot have a beginning without another ending, so the turnover must go on, and everybody needs a break! Some roles onboard are more intense than others, and some people count down the minutes to the end of a contract, while others have to be forced to pack it in. In the 2020 pandemic, when the companies were doing their best to get everyone repatriated, many voluntarily opted to stay onboard instead. In early returns to service, the ship became their bubble of safety. It was the best place in the world to be.

Sign Off

For the end of a contract, the sign-off routine has several stages. You may opt to request an extension or be asked to do so as your replacement may have run into sign-on issues. Once your disembarkation date is actually confirmed, the process begins. You will receive transportation reservations for flights and/or hotels if relevant (this is usually if your flight is *very* early the day after debarkation as the ship will have left the day before). HR will issue several sheets of paper that will need to be signed by various heads of departments to complete your sign-off. These include your department head who will confirm your cabin cleanliness, security for the return of keys, etc.

You will have an assessment from your head of department. This evaluates your performance which includes: timeliness to work, appropriate attire, performance skills, cooperation with fellow crew members, guest comments, cabin etiquette, as well as exceptional performance. Should there be items in the discussion or on the report that you choose to dispute, the conversation will move higher up the chain. This evaluation will have direct repercussions in confirming (or denying) your potential rehire, so it's important to know ahead of time that how you interact with your fellow shipmates can literally allow your shipboard career to sink or swim. As noted in the training section, any tendency to be disruptive or aggressive, get overly inebriated, partake of illegal substances, etc. will have extensive repercussions, both onboard and potentially on land, should an arrest be deemed necessary. These records will follow you worldwide, and possibly for life. *In essence: behave yourself, respect others, and do your job with a spirit of cooperation.* 'Nuff said.

WORK AT SEA, SEE THE WORLD: AN INSIDER'S SECRETS TO THE WORKING LIFE ON A CRUISE SHIP

Oh, No! Packing Again!

So you start packing. Where the hell did all this extra stuff come from? Why won't it fit the way it did when I came? Okay, you collected a few mementos, clothes, a few creature comforts to make your cabin a bit more homey, but now what? In ports, you can always identify the crew members who are signing off soon when they come back from shore leave with new suitcases. When I flew to Hawaii for my first contract, I had to limit my bag to one fifty-pounder. However, returning from Australia on an international flight, I was allowed two bags! A huge relief as not only had my first bag been broken on the flight out, but I also had, of course, amassed a sizable souvenir collection in clothes and other chachkas that necessitated the purchase of a new suitcase. You will always have more stuff than you think you do. There may be a swap chest onboard, where crew can donate their extraneous bits that are too heavy or cumbersome to pack for the benefit of others (that big bottle of shampoo, your yoga mat, etc.), or you may want to leave your comforter and throw pillows (the ones you so excitedly bought at Walmart when you signed on) to your roommate or a friend who is staying onboard.

About three weeks before sign-off, assess the remaining itinerary. If your extras are just a little too big for your bags, there are locations where you can mail packages home. There are always boxes to be found in the incinerator room, and once you have an idea that you won't have room for it, you might want to mail it home. This can be expensive from a foreign port but will get the stuff out of your hair. Or just go ahead and purchase another suitcase and pay for the extra piece (if necessary); it depends on the policy of the airline you are going to fly. This could amount to $35 to $45 (USD) additional, or it may be $100-plus in overweight! Investigate the airline policy online while you still have time to decide, just watch the numbers of pieces allowed and their weight limits. Remember, the company will only cover one bag.

Cleanup

Once you've minimized your stuff in the cabin, you are responsible for thoroughly cleaning it for the next occupant. Deliver your trash to the incinerator room, vacuum the carpet (borrow a machine from a cabin attendant), clean the bathroom, retrieve new linens for the bed and bath from the linen room, wipe down and sanitize everything, and leave it ultraclean for the next guy. It will be inspected and signed off in the paperwork. You will be called to attend a sign-off meeting of all crew disembarking, at which time you will be given forms to sign and evaluations to submit, your last chance to beef about anything you found upsetting. You will drag your luggage down the I-95 to the security area for x-ray, generally before 10:00 p.m. the night before you leave. Be sure to leave out travel clothes and put vital stuff (passport, travel docs, meds, electronics, etc.) in your carry-on bag. The big bags will be loaded onto a crew luggage trolley to be dispatched to the port terminal upon arrival, then held onshore in a separate area awaiting your collection.

Disembarkation

Hopefully you didn't party too late with your buds, as very early the next morning, you will wake up in your very bare cabin. You take all your carry-on luggage to a designated crew area until the HR manager calls on all to go ashore. At that time, you will receive the return of your passport and surrender your crew ID card, cabin key, and emergency card. You will all be ushered through the port terminal together for customs inspection and passport check. After collecting your luggage (carrying everything on your own again—damn, now there's twice as much!), there will be a lot of you from different departments headed to the airport, and there should be a bus provided to get you there.

You settle into the bus seat and watch as this time, it's okay that the ship may be leaving without you. Send her a fond farewell and a bon voyage. You're on your way home with a head full of new adventures, new friends with names you finally learned to pronounce, lots and lots of photos from many new countries, and exposure to folks from places you may have never known existed. You were blessed with an amazing opportunity that a relatively small portion of the population has been able to experience. Yep, there were challenges, but damn it, there was adventure. Congratulations!

Now comes the challenge of readapting to your other life. Wow, will the trials ever end?

CHAPTER 20

So What Happens When It's Over?

Assuming you completed your contract satisfactorily and wish to continue, the company will fly you home. You are usually allotted about a two-month nonpaid vacation. Once you've gotten over the adjustment of being back in your own bed, not feeling the floor moving beneath you, and not having to attend drills or report your hours, you may find it as much of a challenge readjusting to land life as it was to adapt to life at sea. You're happy to be back with family and friends; although some of the latter may have written you out of their lives since you've been gone for so long. Conversations can be challenging as you now have a whole repertoire of stories from your travels, ship life, etc. that others may find hard to understand.

So after all you've experienced, whatcha think? You wanna do it again? I know so many crew members who have served numerous contracts, and every time they sign off, they say, "No, I'm done." But then they had a little time off, they've gotten well rested, the new offer comes in, and they just can't say no! It is not a job for everyone, I admit. If you have a family, that's a whole different story. You don't want to miss your kids growing up and their personal milestones, and leaving your spouse or significant other on their own to bear the burden of family and home care is tough. But there is that detail of the steady paycheck. There are usually those two months of vacation,

WORK AT SEA, SEE THE WORLD: AN INSIDER'S SECRETS TO THE WORKING LIFE ON A CRUISE SHIP

and there is the travel. With FaceTime, Skype, Zoom, WhatsApp, and all the technological advances available as lifelines to home, that electronic connection may fill the personal void as best it can. But you have experienced a world that others could never comprehend.

It may take a while to readjust to having to find things in the grocery store and cooking your own food! But then again, there will be no time clocks to punch; nobody will be calling you on the last day of the month to reprimand you for not finishing your Kronos, making you hop out of bed, and run down the I-95 in your jammies at 2:00 a.m.

Personally I found it the most rewarding and satisfying adventure I could have hoped for. I learned a lot about safety. I learned a lot about ships. I loved my job. I saw some amazing places. I met some awesome people. I gained a sincere empathy for others' situations and made friends in several countries, with whom I still stay in touch years later.

When that call comes again for another contract, what will be your decision? It's up to you. Another adventure awaits. Where will it take you?

CHAPTER 21

Will This Job Help You as a Landlubber?

The following Internet article highlights to employers of land-based jobs the advantages of hiring a cruise ship crew member. Ship life has generally been kept under wraps, and employers are not usually aware of the expansive list of skills that will be developed as crew. You, too, will be able to list these on your résumé, as even one contract on a ship will make you aware of talents and skills you will fully embody as a result of your experiences. And if you find yourself in a position to hire others, you will become more aware of the advantage of these attributes in your application candidates. *(Reprinted with permission of the author.)*

Why Former Cruise Ship Employees Make the Best Employment Candidates
Published on February 3, 2015
By Sean Sassoon

Have you ever worked with or interviewed a former cruise ship employee? If you haven't, then you've missed out on a treat. Crew members and managers from cruise lines offer character traits that are difficult to find in your normal lot of people because employment for a cruise line has a tendency to bring out the best traits in people. Below are just a few examples of how previous employment on ships mold employees into fantastic workers:

***TEAMWORK**—A crew member or manager who has previously worked on ships are serious team players. They have worked in environments where no single employee is responsible for success, but instead the team is. A crew member will often find themselves working in multiple teams, those pertaining to their position, emergency responsibilities, and other situations as they arise. Teams are ever-changing and cruise ship employees have no choice but to adapt to their surroundings and make it work.*

***ADAPTING TO CHANGE**—There are few other jobs that require people to adapt to change as much as working on a cruise ship. Almost daily, managers, supervisors, and crew member's contracts start and end. The people you work with today will almost certainly be different next month, next week, and even tomorrow. Also, while the ship works on a schedule, you have to adapt to the change in itinerary as things arise, in weather, in passenger demographics, and in procedures. You have to be flexible and able to adapt to changes on the fly. One of the first things new employees have to adapt to when joining a ship is changes to their own personal lifestyle.*

***TIME MANAGEMENT**—Cruise line employees are masters of time management. We aren't just talking about how many hours a day one must work. A cruise line employee will often work every day from 4, 6, 8, and even up to 10 months straight without a day off. That doesn't mean that they work non-stop. There are opportunities to take* *a few hours to half a day off from time to time. But most are used to working holidays and weekends. I once interviewed with an employer who asked me if I would be available to work 2–3 extra hours more during a weekday and quite possibly on a weekend from time to time. I responded with "hell yeah! I can do that any time..." The future employer couldn't help but to grin a little as they checked off a box on their interview sheet. Most crew members are also used to working with complex schedules and achieving desired results in quick turnaround times. No matter if it's a Wednesday, Friday night, or Sunday. If the task has to be resolved immediately, it will be done.*

***CONFLICT RESOLUTION**—Often, when working on a ship, employees and managers will face challenges or conflicts. These may occur with passengers, other crew members, and managers. Cruise ship employees know that the passenger, crew member, or manager, aren't going to suddenly disappear without the issue being resolved. Instead, they must address the situation immediately, and attempt to resolve it in the best manner possible. If not resolved in a timely manner, the issue may linger on and become more complex. There are always going to be challenges, but crew members are brilliant at overcoming them.*

***EMPOWERMENT TO LEARN**—Most employees don't join ships expecting that all they have to do is walk across the gangway and start working. There's a process, responsibilities, and things to learn. The knowledge to do your job is not enough. You have to want to learn more and other responsibilities that go along with your job such as safety, security, environmental issues, and yes, job skills. They know that the more skills they learn and* *apply, the better they will do their job. That is why most cruise lines employ permanent trainers and human resource managers and spend money to continually develop training programs for all employees on board.*

***STRESS MANAGEMENT**—When I have told friends and family members that I am leaving to join another ship, they often look at me and say, "You lucky guy." But they have no idea the challenges that employees often have to deal with on board. First, remember that employees do not take their families to work with them on board the ship. They won't see them for months at a time. There are exceptions however, some husbands and wives can work together on the same ship. Crew members often work long hours but remain in full compliance to ILO & MLC laws (International Labor Laws). While some employees may have their own cabins, many don't, depending on their position and the cruise line. While cruise ships do spend money to provide entertainment for crew (Crew Bar, Crew Gym, Crew Mess, Crew Pool, Crew Hot Tub, Crew Events, and Crew Parties), many of the other things you may do at home to relieve stress may be unavailable, which means that you have to be able to adapt to stressful situations on your own. It's because of this, that cruise ship employees are often masters of stress management.*

***INNOVATION**—There's one place that thrives on innovative employees almost daily and that is on a cruise ship. While there are rules and regulations that must be followed to the T, there's also an understanding that innovation is crucial to success. Managers and crew members are always looking for ways to refine a practice or develop better ways to do a job. Often, they must come up with* *solutions that reduce costs, work, and time, without diminishing the end product. Cruise line employees are great observers and often offer the most amazing ideas.*

__DIVERSITY__—There are few other jobs that offer the level of diversity found on board. Diversity comes in a number of forms. Often you will find an average of 60 nationalities from all over the world (Filipino, Italian, American, Chinese, Ukrainian, Mexican, British, Australian, East Indian, South African, etc...) and amazingly they all get along so well. I have to say if there's something I love more than anything else, it's having lunch in the mess. Often, you'll have at least 5 nationalities sitting at your table talking about anything, and the perspectives are brilliant. You have crew from various employment, education, and cultural backgrounds on top of many other forms of diversity, and amazingly enough, they can all work harmoniously together on board a ship. It's because of this exposure to diversity, they are able to accomplish some of the most amazing things.

__CRISIS MANAGEMENT__—So have you watched the news lately? There's almost always something about the cruise industry that makes headlines in the news from accidents, to sickness, to passing through storms. In the end, no matter what happens on board the ship today, the ship must continue to operate tomorrow. Rarely does the operation on a cruise ship come to a halt. When a ship is built, it's expected to run every minute of every hour, 24 hours a day, 365 days a year, for at least 35 years. There are few things that run with that kind of efficiency. On ships, there will always be crisis, from missed ports, to illness, adverse weather, to emergencies that happen at all hours of the night. Crew members are *taught how to deal with crisis, but are also tested often when dealing with them. Crises often create the best employees.*

__SAFETY__—Crew members are extensively trained on safety. Remember, this is no ordinary hotel. It not only floats on water, but also travels to countries all over the world. Safety is a huge part of the operation onboard. It doesn't fall to a select group of people, but in fact safety is everyone's business. Crew members are required to attend pre-departure safety training upon joining their first ship and must continually attend multiple training classes to ensure they fully understand their responsibilities. Aside from training, classes, and drills, crew members are responsible for each other and for the passengers. If they see anything that can be considered a safety hazard, they must report it immediately to their supervisor and are required to submit safety suggestions and report observations daily. Also, because crew consistently attend drills, they will often respond quickly and courageously during a real emergency. Believe me, you want a crew member working on your team.

__RELATIONSHIP BUILDING SKILLS__— Crewmembers are masters of building relationships. Every employee knows that they cannot run the ship on their own and recognize that relationship-building is critical for success. Depending on what kind of position you hold onboard, the type of relationships you build will vary. If you're a stateroom steward, the better the relationship you have with the passengers, the more satisfied they will be, and more money you will receive in tips. If you are a deck officer, you recognize that you will need to build relationships with your other deck and engine personnel. This will make you more successful in managing the *operation of the ship. In the guest relations office, you strive to solve guest issues while turning a complaint into a compliment. Regardless of the position held, working on ships gives you the tools to build long-lasting relationships.*

***TIME OFF**—Generally crew members can work from 3 months to 10 months in a given year without a full day off. Employment on ships is referred to in terms of "contracts" rather than years. Depending on the position held, an employee will work a period of months without a full day off and then will take another period for vacation. This does not mean that employees don't receive time off. They will often leave the ship for several hours at a time in certain ports of call. The industry standard for many employees is to work 6 months on a ship and then to take 6 weeks off. Some cruise lines have shorter contracts like 4 months on and 2 months off, while others have longer contracts where they can work 10 months on and 2 months off. Depending on the operation, a crew member's time off will vary as retail shops, casino, and entertainment departments may have port days off.*

***SICK DAYS & HOLIDAYS**—Once the ship departs from a port, all of these departments will re-open and return to work. If a crew member is sick, they must inform their manager and proceed to the medical facility for evaluation. This serves a number of benefits. First, if a crew member is sick, it reduces the spread of the virus. It also allows the department to plan accordingly to ensure there's sufficient coverage in the work area. They can't exactly bring extra crew on a ship when they are out at sea. Also, it ensures that the crew member has an opportunity to have a speedy recovery. But what most people don't realize is that a ship is staffed with a finite* *number of people in each department, which means that if you're down 1 or 2 crewmembers, your team must work harder. The operation must continue to run as if no one is missing. When dealing with any virus, crew members must stop working and report any symptoms immediately as they may be extremely contagious and could bring the ship to a grinding halt. Crew members have the best work ethic when it comes to using sick days and taking time off. I once interviewed for a land-based job and the employer asked me if I could work occasionally on Saturdays for a few hours. They had no idea that I had just left a ship a few weeks earlier and hadn't had a day off in 6 months. While it is less than ideal to work when sick, most crew will choose to work when they are capable (and not contagious) for the benefit of the team. In extreme circumstances, if a crew member is unable to perform their job for an extended period due to an illness, they may be disembarked to see a specialist or to recover. Depending on the period that they may be away, a replacement might be flown into the next port or the recovered crew member may return to work at the soonest port of call.*

***ON-CALL 24/7**—Yes when you work on a ship, you are essentially on call 24 hours a day, 7 days a week, for months at a time. Many times, you will need to respond to whatever comes your way. This could come in many forms such as drills, emergencies, customer complaints, crew complaints, support, etc. This is one thing most people don't realize when they go to work on a ship for the first time. A lot can happen that requires your attention and the higher you move up in rank of position, the more often you will need to drop what you're doing, roll out of bed, and get right back to work. It's nuts, but* *it becomes your life. After working on a ship, really anything else seems simple in comparison.*

***SMILING CRAMPS**—Yes you heard me right. When working on a ship, you will develop smiling cramps. If you don't, well then, you're not doing your job correctly because smiling is a critical part of your job and often is in your role description. It doesn't only apply to dealing with passengers but also working with your fellow crewmembers. I have never had to smile so much in my life. It's part of the job, but it eventually becomes who you are. You realize that the more you smile, the more friendly you appear to others, the more approachable you are, and the more successful you become, in whatever you end up doing. I have often found that when a crew member leaves a ship after spending months at a time, that most people on land think they are crazy because they smile and greet others much more. This creates the perception that they have in fact had nothing but fun in the time they have spent working on ships. As a result, people are often intrigued, wishing they could work on ships as well. They have no idea that challenges that await them, but the ability to genuinely smile and remain positive no matter what challenge you're dealing with, makes this smiling a skill that you'll learn while onboard, and you will be able to apply almost anywhere.*

***"IT'S NOT MY JOB" IS IRRELEVANT**— One thing you will never or rarely hear onboard a cruise ship is, "It's not my job." It is true that no one on a ship has the skills to do every job, but that's not the point. Regardless of what the issue is, a crewmember will find the answer or at least find someone who has the answer. It's this work ethic that makes employees on ships so successful and valuable. It's the understanding that if the issue isn't resolved, it's not* *going away. It's not like the passenger or crewmember can go to another ship mid-voyage if they are not happy. The problem must be solved or an amicable solution must be found. Constantly being faced with this type of challenge reinforces certain behaviors in crewmembers making them self-starters, multi-taskers, solutions-oriented, and proactive. These are all qualities you would want in any employee and they are often developed in crew members.*

***SELF DEVELOPMENT**—Most crew members are not satisfied just knowing how to do their job. Once they have reached a point where they know their job and they can perform it with ease, they will often take it upon themselves to learn a new job. Cruise lines often have an internal promotions process, so there's always an opportunity for an employee to move up into higher positions and eventually become managers. Almost all of the hotel general managers and captains that you find on ships today have worked their way up from the bottom holding virtually all the jobs in their department until they reached the top. It also makes it easier to accomplish more if you have a firm understanding of the operation on a ship. Most cruise lines have human resources managers and trainers to develop crew so that they become more successful at doing their jobs as well as to help them gain the skills to move up in their careers.*

This is just a handful of the traits that shipboard employees have that makes them so amazing at the work they do. It's rare to find employees in other fields that have the same kind of work ethic that cruise ship employees have. They can handle almost anything that comes their way. I have had the opportunity to work both on and off ships and have to say that working in a land-based job rarely measured up to the daily challenges I have encountered while working on a ship. I would go on further to say, I don't believe I would be as good an employee if it wasn't for my experiences working on board. So next time you speak to or interview an employee who has worked on a ship, remember that their previous work experience may make them more than qualified to handle anything you can throw at them. (Sean Sassoon, Real Estate Associate at Keller Williams Realty)

CHAPTER 22

What Happened to Ships in 2020?

Cruise ships caught a bad rap in the 2020 pandemic situation. As a crew member, although you are hired for one particular job, you are also responsible for helping keep everyone safe from illness onboard. There have always been precautions in place to clean and protect everyone from GI (gastrointestinal illness) or norovirus, but the 2020 coronavirus that spread throughout the world pulled every cruise ship on earth to a halt. Onboard, even under normal sailing circumstances, all crew must be part of the solution with often and thorough sanitization. While landlubbers were stockpiling toilet paper (why?), the big ships were well supplied with 9,600 rolls per week. Illness onboard is most often due to a condition being brought *into* the ship by passengers rather than conditions already there. Every effort is made to preserve the safe bubble.

Sanitation on ships has always been a high priority. Most new ships are equipped with handwashing stations at the food venues, sanitizing gel dispensers everywhere, and cleaning crews are constantly wiping railings, elevators, door handles, etc. Events are scheduled to maintain smooth traffic flow and avoid overcrowding wherever possible. There are degrees assigned to potential hazards referred to as the OPP (Osteopathic Principles and Practice) levels. Level 1 means there are minimal risks, and business runs as usual. Level 2 signifies a "6-in-6," meaning there have been six cases of something reported within six hours, which means there is more cause for concern and heightened awareness and cleanliness. Level 3 is—uh-oh, watch out! At this level, food would be distributed from a crew member wearing gloves (this could be you!). If the ship goes to level 2 or 3, it is everyone's responsibility to help. The shorter cruises tend to be the more hazardous as the clientele is more often young boozers or the elderly who may be more prone to illness. In the aftermath of COVID, the levels were adjusted to include the "ultra" and "ultra plus" for even stricter precautions. Food was only served by specific galley crew, and everyone onboard was required to wear masks at all times (unless actually eating or drinking), and seating in every public area was all social-distanced with chairs blocked off between people.

You may say, "I'm not a cleaner. I'm not doing that!" But frankly, *everybody* is a cleaner! If the guests or crew get sick, the company, the porting countries, or marine regulators can stop the ship from sailing. It makes for massively detrimental publicity, could cost the ship millions of dollars, and it puts a lot of people's health at risk. If you cannot help sanitize, then you cannot work on a ship. Period. Again, put on those big-kid pants and play your part.

WORK AT SEA, SEE THE WORLD: AN INSIDER'S SECRETS TO THE WORKING LIFE ON A CRUISE SHIP

2020

Once the coronavirus was detected, governments and companies of the world were not prepared for such a pandemic (how could they be?). Such a widespread infection hadn't happened since 1919, and it caught everyone by surprise. There were a few cases discovered onboard ships, and this new and contagious virus quickly spread to other guests. Nearly everyone in the world was advised to go home and stay there! There were hundreds of ships on the seas with hundreds of thousands of people onboard around the world. It took tremendous perseverance and patience to get everyone home.

Guests, of course, went first. But as the crew were sent home in phases, some were not allowed into their own countries! Ships were left to drift aimlessly on the various oceans. Periodic dockings were arranged to replenish supplies, and remaining crew members were moved to guest cabins with balcony access as internal ship sanitization efforts progressed.

My friends, Jamaican crew members, were out on a ship in Australia in February of 2020. Their government restricted access as the country insisted that anyone returning to the island be quarantined before rejoining the population. But without the facilities for as many people as had requested entry, those wishing to return had to wait until that space was free. My friends were transported from one ship to another ship, to another ship, until they could get a flight home and were finally quarantined for two weeks before they could rejoin their family.

Ships around the world were left with skeleton crews. But the companies took the time to re-examine their facilities and procedures to comply with what was to become the new normal for service. Crews were put to work deep cleaning the ships inside and out, redesigning and installing ventilation systems to infuse clean air and better circulation, sanitizing all surfaces, and re-evaluating dining and entertainment procedures to allow for social distancing, personal hygiene, and monitoring.

In close cooperation with the Center for Disease Control (CDC), the companies enacted a total revamp of their systems. To leave these hundreds of vessels idle was tremendously expensive, extremely hard on the vessels and equipment, and detrimental to the dedicated public who had become so enamored with this mode of vacation experience. A whole range of protocols were established to enable the industry to return to operation. The ships were ordered to be out of service beginning March 2020. With tremendous changes and extensive analysis, ten months later, some ships were allowed to try again.

Back to Service? The Revival Story

It wasn't until November of 2020 that there appeared to be a hope of recovery for the beleaguered cruise industry. I was working as a contractor aboard the first ship to attempt a return to service. One of the few countries that seemed to have the virus contained was Singapore. Government mandates had been enacted early to require the wearing of masks, and a regular biweekly system of testing had managed to contain exposure. The only cases detected came in from travelers from other countries, so immigration requirements were enacted for strict pretravel quarantine, extensive testing, and controlled travel within the country.

To comply with the directive, I was isolated in a quarantined hotel room in Miami for two weeks. Food was delivered for breakfast, lunch, and dinner. I took time to write, Zoom with friends, and read. I also tried to maintain an exercise schedule as best I could by tuning in to online workout classes. I calculated the number of laps from the window to the door and formulated an equivalent to miles…hmm…197 laps to a mile? That never happened.

In preparation for admission to Singapore, there was a plethora of forms and questionnaires to complete. We were temperature-tested every day and given a PCR test at the end of the fourteen days. We were taken to the cruise port where we met with a doctor who signed off on our fit-to-fly documents. The next day, we were bussed to the Miami airport.

At the check-in counter, a *long* QR-coded questionnaire had to be completed to get a boarding pass and allow baggage check. On the plane, the socially distanced seating arrangement gave me the center four seats of the plane to myself on this nine-hour flight. We arrived in London at 8:00 a.m. local time and had eleven hours to kill before the connecting flight. Wearing the ever-present mask and maintaining social distancing as best we could, I looked longingly at the souvenir postcards of Big Ben and Parliament that I wished I could visit in this extended time period, but leaving the terminal was not allowed as it would invalidate our two weeks of quarantine!

On the next flight, again I lucked out with three seats to myself for the thirteen-hour flight. We arrived at 7:00 p.m. and were met by a ship agent at the gate in the beautiful Singapore airport full of glass, sculpture, and huge plants and escorted to the immigration area. Again there was an enormous list of forms that all needed to be completed on our smartphones in order to be admitted. One by one, we were fed into the immigration line for photos and fingerprints before we were let out of the chutes to collect our luggage. There were hardly any other people in the airport, and we were finally ushered to a waiting bus. Emerging from the air-conditioned terminal, we were enveloped in warmth and humidity, even though it was about 9:00 p.m. in mid-November. The town seemed ghostly with minimal traffic and no pedestrians.

Arriving at the marina, from level 1 of the parking garage, we herded our stuff into the elevators to level 3 to endure more testing. Socially distanced plastic chairs were prepared for our arrival in several sections. Showing my passport, I was given a sheet of identification labels. Progressing to another set of chairs, the next phase was a PCR test conducted by a nurse in full protective gear sticking a swab up both my nostrils that scrambled my brain (ouch)—two labels used up. Remask. Next stop, the blood-draw station to be poked in the arm with a syringe (ouch again)—two more labels. Blowing my nose and massaging my arm, but freed at last, I retrieved my luggage and went back down the elevators to the main terminal entrance. Passport check again, then drag the luggage over the carpet (gee, has anyone ever calculated the coefficient of a fifty-pound bag on tile versus carpet?) to yet another x-ray machine. Alley up that weight to have them all scanned and proceed through an airport-style metal detector. Any alcohol? Nope. Any tobacco? Nope.

Continuing through the terminal, there was yet another immigration gate for even more photos, more fingerprints, more document checking, until cleared at last to board. Then it was up a switchback gangway. I was given rubber gloves and asked to step into a litter-box pan of chemically soaked towels to clean shoes, then I herded everything down the deck where the luggage was fogged for sanitization. Once allowed inside the ship, a table of hazmat-attired medical crew examined documents, collected passports and forms, performed a temperature check, and issued cabin keys.

I was assigned a quarantine area guest cabin on deck 8. We had boarded at the gangway aft, and of course, my cabin was nearly all the way forward. *OMG—more freaking carpet!* It took two trips, but the extra steps were good for me after all that airplane sitting. There was a tiny table outside with a plastic box of cold dinner, a bag of chips, a pack of cookies, and a case of water. Once I had dragged it all inside, I picked over the cold dinner and assessed the situation. I had an unmade bed to assemble, but whew, I had made it!

As the ship was still operating with minimal crew, the food came from an outside vendor. The plastic boxes were delivered three times a day, but the food was cold by the time it arrived. After a knock at the door, it was left on the table outside with a plastic bag. After finishing the meal, any leftover food was to be dumped into the bag and left outside with the empty box.

We were allowed three hours of free Wi-Fi, which enabled completion of some of the online crew training required. I settled into a routine and was pretty darn comfortable. I enjoyed my balcony view of the harbor. But then a surprise! On the evening of day 5, the phone rang. It was the ship's doctor. "Pack up," he said, "You have to leave the ship."

What? "Why?" I asked incredulously.

"Just pack!" was the curt replay. "Be ready in half an hour."

A pounding on my door revealed an insistent crew member, in full hazmat gear, who handed me a bag containing the same: a white paper hazmat suit, an N95 mask, blue shoe booties, and a clear plastic face shield. Hmm, was I being protected from the outside world or was it being protected from me? Probably both. Either way, I was in my own safe little bubble. These guys were so conscientious and determined to keep everyone safe! I was escorted from my cabin (oh geez, here we go again with the damn carpeting!) to the gangway. There were five of us, all identically attired as we were ushered off the ship. Our passports were returned, and we were loaded onto a bus, keeping social distance, and driven through the spooky, empty, and darkened streets to a Singapore hotel. There was an obvious hush among us as we wondered where the heck we were going and the gravity of the precautions set in. Were we done before we'd even begun? Having received minimal explanations, our trepidations were obvious.

We were unloaded behind the hotel at the base of the parking garage, and we had to drag our bags up one level. I was hyperventilating in the suffocating mask and suit amid the heat and humidity still lingering at 9:00 p.m. At the top of the ramp, we were spaced out on wooden chairs to wait our turn for the attention of the admitting team. One by one, we were called forward, and we whispered to each other, curious as to why they needed to rummage through our bags.

"So what are you looking for? I can tell you where it is!" I blurted out as my anxious voice echoed through the concrete garage.

"Any alcohol, cigarettes, and chewing gum…and anything sharp, even nail clippers," was the terse reply. I relinquished scissors, and I had to wonder if they thought our confinement was going to be so traumatic that we might harm ourselves!

Once I was ushered to my room, a tracking band was wrapped onto my wrist. An electronic box in the room would notify authorities should the tracker indicate that I had left the room without authorization. Such actions would, of course, invalidate all the time served already and be pointless. Aha, that's why nothing with which to cut, and where would I go anyway?

Confined to my room, a metal TV tray blocked the door for the delivery of meals. The room was comfortable enough, a simple Asian-inspired decor in black and brown, with tiled floor and a large platform bed. But the view from the window was the wall of the adjoining building. I could just peek out to see the sky above. A ringing doorbell signaled meal deliveries as the attendant scampered away. I was given a choice of cuisine between Chinese, Halal, Indian, or Western, and much as I would have liked to experience some local fare, it didn't seem the time to mess with the digestive balance. Opting for Western, the food was pretty tasty. We had been given an oral thermometer, and twice a day, the phone rang so that we could report our temperature readings to the Office of the Minister of Health. They at least trusted us that far to be honest!

The TV channels were mostly in Chinese and Hindi, but there was one movie channel of American action films (Vin Diesel, Dwayne Johnson, Arnold Schwarzenegger, etc.) and a Singapore/World News channel in English. But whoo-hoo, there was free unlimited Wi-Fi, so online entertainment was the go-to. And since I didn't have a power converter for the laptop, all I could charge from the USB port was my phone, so all I could manage was tiny little streaming movies!

Twice I was escorted from my room and taken for a scenic drive through the now-bustling city in my own taxi with a hazmat-attired driver, who kept the windows open. It was fun to watch the speedometer climb to over one hundred…kilometers! An open-air school had been converted to a PCR-testing station. After enjoying the return taxi tour of the city, I was again shuffled in through the back door of the hotel and up the service elevator to isolation. The remaining required nine quarantine days ran out at last. We were all given a negative test from our excursion. The confiscated items were returned, and we were escorted to the lobby, which we had never seen! After an extended wait, finally a bus arrived to take us back to the ship.

This time, we were allowed directly into the terminal. Here we go again with the x-rays. But hold on! We were not allowed onboard just yet. Apparently the Singapore Ministry of Health does not issue paper documentation of the negative test results, and the ship doctor was loath to allow anyone who had "been outside" into his safe-ship bubble. The security staff brought us a McDonald's lunch and again, hurry up and wait. Four hours later, as folks in Miami awoke, the captain could secure corporate authorization, and we were allowed to proceed. Here we go with the whole immigration process again—

pics, prints, fogging, etc.—and were given a key to our original quarantine cabins. Hello, carpet.

"My" room had been completely cleaned and now prepared for guests, and I felt guilty messing up the now neatly made bed! In the morning, we learned that there had been debate about returning us to quarantine status (c'mon, it's been more than four weeks already!), but the office in Miami managed to quell the concerns of the doctor, and we were allowed to move to our permanent cabins. This meant moving everything to the other end of the ship, from deck 8 down to deck 3, but it had to be done all in one trip. Hello, dreaded carpet, *again*!

Freedom at last! Once relocated, I cruised the ship and marveled at the magnificent view of the Singapore skyline. It seems that we had been "C-sectioned from our ship womb" because someone had tested positive somewhere near us at the airport. It took five days of security camera scrutiny to track down who we were and where we had gone. Although we were already completely sequestered, the government seemed to need to be in control of the rest of our quarantine and testing.

The new ship protocols required the tracking of everyone's movements to isolate any potential issues. In addition to our ID cards, we were outfitted with a "tracelet" wrist tracker for the company, as well as another transmitter for the Singapore government. We had to report for a temperature check twice each day. Every venue onboard was equipped with a tracking pad where an entrant's ID was recorded, and another temperature check was required before being allowed to pass. Once all crew were released from quarantine, there was a test run of procedures before paying guests were allowed. Only seven hundred corporate folks came aboard for a simulation cruise for monitoring, then we would be allowed to launch revenue cruises to gradually increase capacity to a maximum of 50 percent.

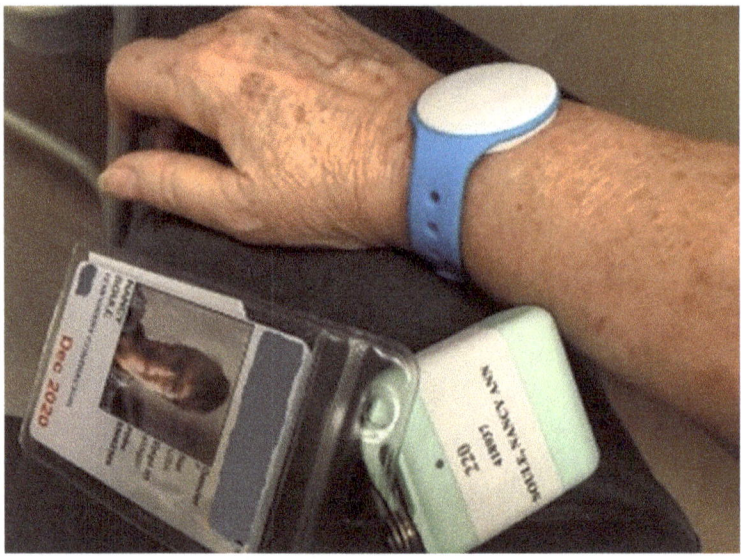

At last, the entertainment venues were allowed to open. Musicians played behind plexiglass shields, but no one was allowed to dance or sing along. Performers were now "concertizing" rather than encouraging participation. And there was no alcohol served in the performance venues, as drinking would require removal of masks; a tough gig for the pub entertainer who usually relies on a rowdy crowd but who now played solo to a room of staring eyes!

But the first shakedown cruise went off without a hitch. Everyone arriving and leaving was tested, as were crew each week, and all reported negative results, and the green light was given to continue! The next cruise was 1,200 guests. The itinerary of trips to nowhere alternated between three and four-day cruises. We left port and just "drove around" in the ocean.

WORK AT SEA, SEE THE WORLD: AN INSIDER'S SECRETS TO THE WORKING LIFE ON A CRUISE SHIP

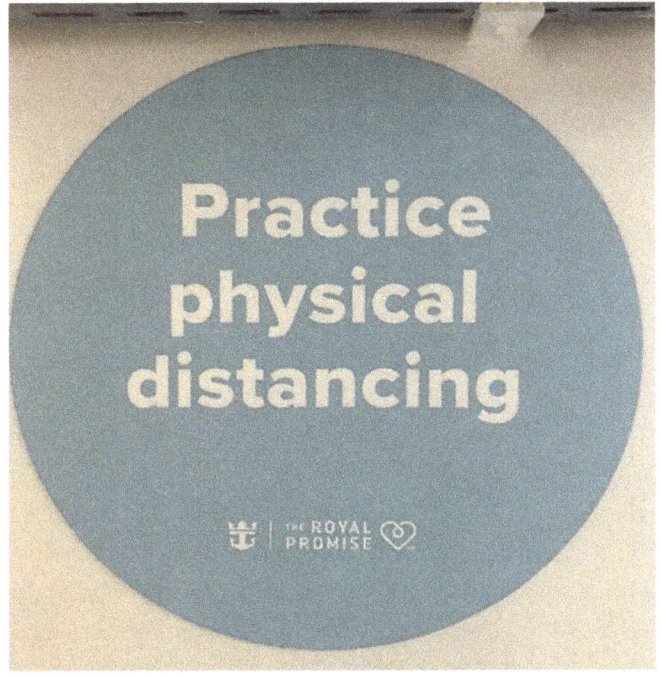

On day two of the second four-day, we were out at sea, running at about nine knots, when there was the captain calmly announced a report of an eighty-three-year-old gentleman who had become ill. We were requested to abide by the protocol, stay in our cabins, and temporarily self-isolate while we headed back to port. Meals were delivered efficiently, and the guests spent the last day of the cruise enjoying the splendor of their comfortable cabins. On our return to port, the gentleman in question and his family were disembarked, as were several crew members who had worked in his vicinity, as a precaution. The guests were tested, all were reported negative, and they were carefully disembarked by family group. We proceeded to resanitize, fog hallways, etc. In the meantime, the gentleman in question had had further tests and found that he, too, was actually proven negative for COVID after all. But the next three-day cruise was cancelled to allow for further cleansing of the ship.

Frankly it gave the crew a chance to breathe! Everyone had been so on edge, so extremely careful of every move, following the guidelines to the letter. With the negative tests, there was a cumulative sigh of relief and encouragement that we had been doing everything right after all! For the next cruise, we were given the green light for a group of 1,750 guests.

The new-normal capacity (50 percent of maximum or about two thousand guests) was achieved. The protocols had been tried and tested, and the procedures were approved. Whew! There is hope for the future after all! As vaccinations rolled out worldwide, the potential for full return to service got underway as more ships in the fleet and other companies followed suit. I continue to endure quarantines in preparation for getting ships back to service until the cruise world is restored to its full operation. In my experience, quarantine durations have been drastically reduced, and each ship has different procedures. But the pandemic provided tremendous opportunities for improvements that have contributed many positives to the industry.

The following article was posted in the http://www.crew-center.com website in October 2021. As quarantines might still be part of the process, I include an edited version as a potential guide to onboard isolation survival.

Let out, but locked in: *A Survival Guide to Cruise Ship Quarantine* by Nancy Soulé

So, it's been a long time since the 1975 movie *Jaws* was released, but "just when you thought it was safe to go back in the water..." we all wonder if we are really safe from the Covid shark that lurks in the deep (and it's subsequent variants). As the cruise ship industry begins to return to service, extensive health protocols have been put in place to protect everyone as best they can. It's a good thing we've got "a bigger boat!" But, for the foreseeable future, anyone working onboard in excess of 30 days must endure the mandatory period of 7 to 14 days in quarantine. This could be perceived as prison or vacation! It's all in your perspective. Confined to a single room, the physical and mental hurdles may be difficult to manage without some preparation. Having endured many of these quarantines, I offer the following as suggestions for your survival.

Some companies may require vaccination, but others may provide it once onboard. At least 72 hours before departure, you will need to complete a PCR test and secure paperwork to prove a negative result. This can often be done at a local urgent care or one of your local medical facilities. Transportation to the port will probably be arranged by your company, and sign-on procedures will vary depending on the state of service of the ship. Some, if just reviving from an extensive hibernation, will be in the early processes. The only crew onboard ahead of you may be those handling basic operational deck service, medical staff, and some culinary teams to feed everyone. Health staff will be on hand at boarding to scrutinize medicals, perform temperature checks and PCR or Antigen tests. If you have been vaccinated, be sure that card is completed and ready; they will make a copy of it for their records.

Once onboard, staterooms are in a segregated guest area of the ship marked with signage to indicate that admittance is only by authorized personnel. So, is this prison or a vacation? Well, by all appearances, this may look like the latter. You have been assigned a comfortable and spacious guest stateroom with a large king-sized bed, a sofa, a desk, a large closet, a big dresser, and…a balcony! Wow! Time to play "guest!" There may also be a bar cooler. Depending on how long this ship has been left idol, that last item may or may not be in cooling condition. But if it is, and you planned ahead, this little appliance could be a lifesaver. If yours is malfunctioning, call maintenance immediately and they may loan you a portable "special needs" cooler before you are officially "locked in."

Here are a few suggestions. Be aware that there may be a couple of extra days before release.

Food. You will probably be asked to scan a QR code on paper or tv for menu selection, but the descriptions are very brief, and included some ethnic dishes with names about which I didn't have a clue. You may have to guess a lot. Mine had allowances for vegan and vegetarian options.

Onboard, breakfast generally was delivered around 7:30 am, lunch about 12:30, and dinner at 6:30. You may have the option to order more than one meal if you're really hungry, and my digital menu asked if I would like extra rice or bread, and my beverage choices were coffee, tea, milk, and/or juice. You should receive at least one case of bottled water, sometimes two. Your cabin might be equipped with a hot water kettle. If you have a favorite instant coffee or tea, bring some. Ah the joys of a guest cabin! You may also be allowed to order snacks from the slop chest with a small credit allowance—you will still have to pay when you get out though.

When my first experience onboard was over, I found I had put on an extra 15 pounds of weight as the diet seemed loaded with bread, potatoes, rice, as well as lots of sugar in desserts, sauces, and salad dressings. At the conclusion of the first contract, I was horrified at the readings on the scale and was determined to reverse the situation. When I got home, I spent the next three months consumed with dieting to get it off. For the next ship, I vowed that I would skip the bread, potatoes, rice, and sugar as much as possible, and that seems to work pretty well to stay even. However, I must admit that the occasional servings of French fries and chocolate mousse somehow slipped through the cracks in my resolve. Oops. And I went just a little crazy with the choices post-quarantine with the ice cream and pizza, but I didn't gain anything back and tried to stick to salads often.

So, in preparation for ship quarantine #2, I packed my suitcase with food to bridge the time gaps and provide some lower calorie snacks. It took some careful weighing to stay under plane regulations, but the bags were much lighter coming home. Subsequent contracts allowed for a quick grocery stop enroute to the ship. These are just my personal choices:

a. Raw almonds.
b. SkinnyPop popcorn. A large bag can be divided into about 7 quart-size zip-lock bags that will keep it fresh and meter out the consumption.
c. Almond butter. Choose a natural smooth-blend brand with minimal oil that won't separate such as Barney Butter, which does not require refrigeration, and won't leak in your luggage.
d. Canned olives. Black or green, whole or sliced, in pull-top cans or snack-size prepared servings.
e. Dark Chocolate. Who can live without this? I meter the squares out carefully to make them last as long as possible. Nice to mix with a few raw almonds.

Try to avoid excessively high-fat, processed, high-salt snacks and remember to drink A LOT of water. Call room service if you need help or want extra food delivered; hopefully they will accommodate you.

Utensils. Meals are delivered in either paper compostable or plastic boxes (thereafter recycled) and utensils are plastic. I recommend that you bring your own utensils and a napkin. The compostable boxes sometimes would bleed if the food was too liquid, so a small plastic cutting board was helpful to put under the box when I wanted to dine from the comfort of my bed while watching tv without worrying about leaking red spaghetti sauce onto my fresh white duvet.

Clothing. Remember, the only people who will see you are the daily temperature check person, maybe an occasional food delivery staff, or possibly your neighbor as you retrieve your meals. Comfort is the primary concern. You can control the temperature of your cabin. I spend my days in sweatpants and have two or three tees. I take slippers because my feet get cold when I sit too long on the computer or watching tv. I'd rather not have to wash socks...yoga and stretching are easily done in bare feet.

Laundry. Speaking of socks, laundry may be done in your bathroom sink, or taken with you into the shower. Liquid soap or shampoo work well. Liquid laundry pods run the risk of breaking in your luggage, so an alternative is powdered pods, soap flakes, or laundry sheets.

Exercise. Being locked in one room, the lure of tv programs and phone/computer games may sidetrack your intentions toward maintaining a fitness schedule and give only your thumbs a workout. If you have good and extensive Wi-fi, there are plenty of online classes to suit any fitness level, but better to use your own downloads. Here are some tools that will help:

- a. Stretch or Pilates bands. The ones with handles can be looped over a wall hook or wrapped around a bed leg for various moves.
- b. Water bottles. You will probably get a case to start. After I've drunk the fresh water from the bottles, the 1.5L ones can be refilled with tap water and lashed together with stretchy bands to make weights.

c. Laptop. Recorded exercise routines give me someone to follow.
d. Twister. A "Figure Trimmer" is a fun little disc for waist/ab work (Amazon). About a foot in diameter, it weighs only a pound. With bearings in the middle and acupressure points under your feet, you can twist as long as you like while watching tv and whittle that waistline or work on your lats. Best when the ship's not moving too much!
e. Floor discs. These flat little discs (by Bally) have fabric for hard floors on one side and plastic on the other for use on carpets. Placing your toes on them, you can do ab work like mountain climbers, side twists, or with hands, can work abs by pulling them in/out when on your knees. Handy and easily packable.
f. Wall sitting. Good for abs and legs and requires no tools.
g. Planks. You should have enough room to work those abs.
h. Dance. Turn on your tunes or the music video channel on the television, and DANCE for as long as you can!

WORK AT SEA, SEE THE WORLD: AN INSIDER'S SECRETS TO THE WORKING LIFE ON A CRUISE SHIP

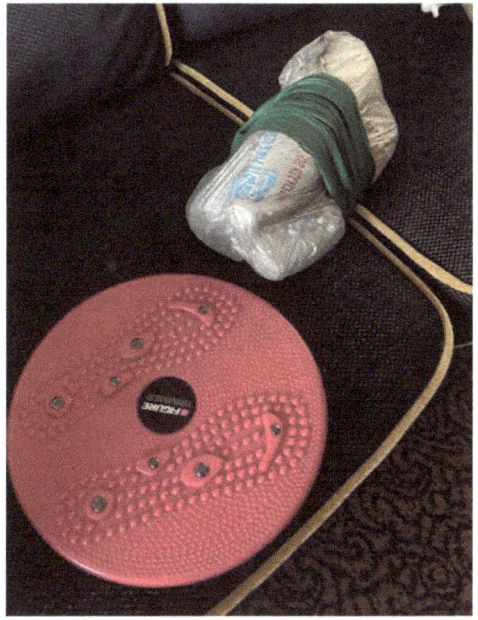

Electronics:

a. A cell phone is a given—nobody can survive without one for basic communication. Onboard, some crew trainings, quarantine menus, and important communication from human resources are available.

b. A light-weight laptop will provide workspace and entertainment. Take an additional hard drive for larger files and downloaded movies. In quarantine, depending on the company, you may have Wi-fi available in various durations. Speed may differ, and I've found live Zooms are easier to connect to than replays that take a while to load. Pull yourself away from Facebook for a while and take advantage of the chance

to do online courses or learn something on Youtube.
c. Cords for charging everything.
d. A 6 to 10-foot phone charging cord.
e. A 6-foot non-grounded extension cord. Most outlets are not near the bed. Security frowns on power strips, but a wimpy one like this is usually ok.
f. A multi-USB hub will facilitate connecting phone, computer, earbuds, etc. at the same time.

Other items:

a. Analogue clock. As the plugs are limited, a battery-operated clock allows for easy adjustment as ship location demands periodic time changes. Nice to have something visible to help you anticipate the joys of meal delivery.
b. Sleep mask. Curtains are usually "blackout" material, but don't always close completely. Wherever your destination, with no specific need to get up early, the sun may have other ideas. An eye mask will help you block it out until you're ready to get up. That 7am breakfast knock might get you going though.
c. Chip clip. In the same vein, a chip clip or clothes pin will help you secure the curtains.

Quarantine can be a chance to chill out and reconnect with yourself without the demands of work schedules or family obligations. Relish the time. It will be over before you know it. So, consider this as an opportunity and not a requirement. Once returned to "general population" you may find yourself back in either a single or a shared crew cabin...no balcony, no window, maybe minimal privacy. Enjoy it while you can! Try to turn off the tv and electronics and enjoy the opportunity for some introspection. Plan, dream, imagine, pray, meditate, whatever your creative brain wants to do that your daily "busyness" may have prevented. This is YOUR time—enjoy it!

Just remember that once you are "out" it is vital to maintain compliance with the protocols: masks, ID scans, social distancing as much as possible among both crew and guests. Sorry, no cabin parties. The shark still lurks, so try to stay out of its way. This situation will end eventually, and we're literally all in the same boat. Be sensible and take care of each other.

Quarantine procedures proved effective at keeping people safe, and the amount of time required for new sign-ons changed as time went on. From the four weeks in preparation for the Singapore start-up, the duration went to fourteen days, then ten, then three. As service tries to return to the "old normal," the "new normal" has aspects that might stay for a while. Slowly, the mask requirements may be loosened, and the vaccination requirements may change. Time will tell.

The industry has finally loosened up restrictions on testing and masks, but beware of resurgence. Cases are lessening, but may still require limited quarantine isolation. Now you are prepared "just in case!"

You may decide to go back to the land life. To do so, here are some things to keep in mind should those telltales prompt you to tack in another direction.

CHAPTER 23

So What to Do Next?

How to Manage the Afterlife

So there you have it: everything I can think of that would be helpful to know if you are considering a job on a ship. At sea, time can stand still, and your contract will be over before you know it. But the life skills you have amassed have taught you habits that will make you even more valuable to any other employer as well. You've seen the plethora of skills that will serve you in your "afterlife" from sea duty and can expand your work opportunities.

But don't take my word for it all. Here are some after comments about life on land to consider from Mackenzie Ames from her blog on the subject. (*Reprinted with permission of the author.*)

**I've Got a Lovely Bunch of Coconuts;
9 Things No One Tells You About Moving to Land**
Thoughts From a Landlocked Sailor
By Mackenzie Ames; *Lovelycoconuts.wordpress.com*
September 10, 2014

> Your friends and family will be so happy to hear that you're finally leaving that crazy ship life, but there are definitely things about land life they want to keep secret for fear you'll change your

mind. I'm going to let you in on the diabolical plan.

1. **Finding A Job Is So Hard.**

I'm from the class of 2009. You know, the class with the headline, "Worst Job Market Since the Depression For Graduates." Getting a job on the ship was quick and kind of easy, so when I quit, I thought it would only be a matter of weeks before I would have a new gig lined up. I already had work experience so it should be a piece of cake, right? WRONG! I was unemployed for 8 MONTHS before finding my current job.

2. **Conference Calls Suck.**

I am incredibly spoiled. My break room was the beach. My lunch was a picnic in Copenhagen, and if we ever had meetings, it was in the staff mess over a couple beers. Y'all, office life is pretty boring. Conference calls are the worst. Land people neglected to tell me the groan I would release with every "Meeting Invite" email I would receive.

3. **Living Alone Feels Strange.**

I don't know about you guys, but when I would come home from my contracts, I found that I would rarely leave my bedroom. I would eat, watch tv, play on my laptop and everything else in my room. I came to realize that after living in a tiny cabin for so long, I was more comfortable in the smallest room I could find. Strange, huh? When I finally got my own place, I started to feel really lonely. I wasn't surrounded by friends along my hallway anymore. My closest friend was at least an hour away. I was definitely feeling the effects of the friendship claw.

4. **Travel Is Really Expensive.**

Oh my God! It costs how much for a plane ticket to England!? Guess I won't be seeing my British friends for a while. When traveling is your job, you lose all perspective on how costly transportation is.

5. **Have A Great Vacay! See You In Three Days!**

Also, can we talk about how impossible it is to make 10 days of vacation last for the whole year? Crew members typically get to go home for 1–2 months. Having a couple months was ideal for checking off family visits, catching up with friends, having a crazy weekend or two and then heading back to work.

6. **Dressing Up Only Happens On Halloween.**

Sadly, land people don't throw theme parties at the drop of a hat. All my costume creativity has gone to waste here.

7. **You're Hired! Now Go Buy A New Wardrobe.**

They do, however, dress up for work. Your new job will probably not give you a uniform to wear, and those sundresses you bought in St. Maarten aren't considered "office appropriate." Get ready to drop some cash on blouses and pencil skirts. Or you can be like me and wear tights a lot. Not sorry. Don't care.

8. **Designated Drivers Is A Thing You Have To Remember.**

Unless you are lucky enough to move to a big city after ships (which is probably helpful at alleviating a couple of these rude awakenings), walking upstairs to your room after the bar isn't a thing anymore. Now you have to be responsible and decide which of your friends is going to have a miserable night. Trust me when I say the "oh I totally forgot you have to have a DD on land" excuse won't fly for long with your new land-lubbing friends.

9. **Somehow You Work Less and Are Tired More.**

On ships you work some of the longest hours of your life and somehow, you're always up for a night out afterward. When you move to land you will work less hours but be way more exhausted than ever before. Remember how you used to stay up until 1 am and then be in your office by 8 am the next day. Remember how you did this like, every day? On land you'll work for eight hours, make dinner, watch like one show on Netflix and feel ready for bed by 9:30 pm. Weekend? You might make it to 10:30 pm.

I am glad I made the move to land. I have no regrets about my decision, but I'm on to you land people. You sneaky folks with your deception want us poor sailors to think the seaweed is greener in somebody else's lake. Well, I'm not falling for it. Yea, you've got a whole bunch more freedom, and no inane rules about flips flops, and the ability to make whatever you want for dinner, but I see the game you play.

Be warned, ship friends. Be warned.

I am just a girl who misses the saltwater in her hair...wait is that dirty? Crap. I always try to sound so elegant and profound and it just ends up warranting some prepubescent chuckle.

I lived on a cruise ship for three years and am adjusting to land life again. I have changed. I am sorting through these changes here for my friends,

WORK AT SEA, SEE THE WORLD: AN INSIDER'S SECRETS TO THE WORKING LIFE ON A CRUISE SHIP

family and the world to read. Slowly realizing there is nothing in the world like ship life...and that's ok.
Follow me on Twitter: @mackenzieames
Drop me a line: landlocked.sailor25@gmail.com

And another note from Mackenzie:

VITAL INFORMATION for the GIRLS!

Sorry gentlemen, but I need to talk to my sisters for a sec. Ship life can be scary and overwhelming, and there are certain warnings I think women need to hear before walking up that gangway. So pop on some Beyonce and let me give you the 411.

Being Taken Seriously Is Difficult

Unfortunately, today you will almost always wonder if your gender is affecting you career. It probably is. I know it affects mine. On a ship it completely works against you. Getting American men to take you seriously in a place of authority is difficult enough, but try doing it with men who aren't accustomed to working with women in their home countries. Some of them will insist on you letting them do everything. You would think that sounds pretty nice, until you realize it's cause they think the fragile female creature can't perform heavy lifting or operate power tools. You'll also have to deal with the fact that men from certain parts of the world do not want to work with women—and they just won't. Be prepared to have men look past you and speak to you like they are reprimanding their daughter.

Tampons Are Sold in Like the Weirdest Places

Tampax are not universally sold, and if they are they're usually expensive. Maybe stock up before you leave. If you're in a bind, though, and stuck at sea for days you can always go buy a box from the gift shops. You know, from that guy you'll probably see at the bar tonight. Or even better! You can walk into the staff bar, make your way through the small crowd of men, and buy your tampons along with your Pringles and a Heineken. They're literally behind the bar with everything else. Talk about one stop shop… Gross.

There Will Be Creepers

Oh my Gosh, no matter what you do there will be men who stare at your nametag for too long and slip unwanted gifts under your door. I had one creeper follow my boyfriend and me around the crew bar all night. Didn't matter if the boyfriend and I were holding hands, kissing or I was sitting on his lap, the creeper still followed us like he was waiting. Don't be mean to men onboard, but be careful. Some of them get stalker-y. Also, if a guy asks you to "watch a movie" or "see pictures on his computer," he wants in your pants. Certain nationalities have their own tricks of the trade, but that one's a dead giveaway. You have been warned.

There Will Be Cheaters

Be prepared to see a shit ton of cheating. Men will have wives onboard one week, and a dancer in his bed the next week. I'm not saying it's right, just get used to it happening all the time. And stay away from all that. Ship life generates enough drama on its own, don't go seeking it out.

Sometimes the Uniforms Are Not Made for You

You mean I get to wear poly-blend polos worn by men who just signed off?? Seriously, they say they're handing you ladies uniforms, but my cargo pants were definitely not meant for my figure. It just feels like nothing is cut for a woman's body. If you can, find out if wearing your own professional attire is allowed.

Don't Bring Too Many Clothes, Especially in the Carib

Speaking of clothes, ladies refer to the packing list, and try to remember if you're going to the Caribbean, you'll basically be living in a bathing suit, tank tops and shorts. Bring more than one bathing suit, in case you're one from the day before is still wet.

Know Where in the World You Are

There are certain ports of call where no matter what your inner feminist tells you, you can't venture out by yourself (I'm looking at you, Cairo). Be educated on where you are in the world. Know if there is hostility toward women where you are and if it might be smarter for you to bring a male friend. It's not weak, it's smart.

Have Your Own Box of Condoms

I can't stress this enough. Safe sex is up to both parties. There are a lot of men from cultures that "don't like" using condoms so they never bring one. Have your own stashed in your nightstand and be prepared for him to argue about having to use it. Stay strong. No glove, no love.

Wash Your Own Clothes

Ok, so there's a crew laundry that you can pay for and someone washes and folds your clothes for you. Girls, be careful! I strongly suggest washing your panties in your own sink, unless you want some of them to mysteriously disappear. Seriously. It has happened to more than one friend of mine. Also, on most ships there are washer and dryers for you to use, sometimes you just have to search for them and be ok with there being like one for a whole floor of cabins. If this is the case, you better be there to get your clothes right when that dryer is done. Most of the time someone will just put all your clean clothes on the floor, but in some cases girls will steal your clothes. And in some other cases, dumbass girls will wear your clothes to the bar while you're still onboard. Stupid criminals…

You Need to Stick Together

This is the most important thing for girls onboard to remember, and the hardest one to live by. Women are vastly outnumbered onboard and you would think that would mean we would join together in solidarity, but when has anything ever stopped the power of cliques? Don't let the dramas and frustration of men and ship life pull you apart. There are already so few of you, don't alienate more of them. Ship life can be pretty lonely without your girlfriends.

Check online for additional blogs from Mackenzie Ames at: www.lovelycoconuts.wordpress.com

"How Ship Life is like Summer Camp"
"How Ship Life is like College"
"How Ship Life is like Prison"
"How Ship Life is like Dirty Dancing"
"Mean Girls explain Ship Life"

Still thinking about it? So, are you still game for the adventure? As you can see, everybody has their own feelings about having worked on a ship, but I thought you might be interested in these comments from fellow crewmembers. The following was submitted by crewmember Debasis Sarkar of West Bengal; This is his take on life on board:

"To remind you of the ship life..."

- Days of the week become countries.
- You have to turn on the TV to see the weather outside.
- When almost every night, as soon as you close your eyes, the alarm goes off.
- Happy hour can be any hour you're not working.
- Where you can get drink for a few dollars or less in the crew bar.
- Hangovers can be blamed on seasickness.
- Hours back determine when parties are on. (frequent time zone changes)
- You haven't had 10 minutes alone since you arrived onboard.

- You've walked into your cabin, your cabin mate seems to be naked, and you can't unsee it.
- Arriving in a new country, usually feeling asleep, and finding food, beer and Wi-fi.
- Having a liquid lunch in the crew bar.
- You haven't known what day of the week it is for 8 months.
- Working less than 10 hours is considered to be "an easy day".
- Partying with your bosses is not unusual.
- It has been 4 days since you've stepped outside.
- You've just spent a 16-hour sea day with the same people, go to dinner and then happily spend the rest of the night in the crew bar.
- Seeing the captain at the gym is like seeing a movie star at the supermarket.
- You smile even if you're having a bad day.
- You're so far from home, but seem to be surrounded by your family.
- You'll be used to using a tiny bathroom and you can sit on toilet and brush your teeth at the same time!
- When you talk about how to spend your time off it's in terms of "hours off" not "days off".
- Packing is a nightmare.
- You can survive with one piece of luggage full of clothes for 8 months but then you'll need to buy a bigger luggage for all the stuff you've bought.

- When you get back home, you'll call your room a cabin, and feel naked without a name badge.
- When you're in the real world you have to stop yourself from saying hello to random people passing on the road.

10 advantages to being a crewmember:

1. Crew discounts in the ports. Often the ports where the ships dock are happy to allow the crewmembers either a discount on purchases or free admission to cultural attractions such as museums or wildlife sanctuaries. Always ask!
2. Some places even have specific beaches allotted for crew. Many ports have special CrewCenters where you can get inexpensive Wi-fi, electronics, and sundries, ethnic foods, and a place to hang out on land. They may be within walking distance or provide a shuttle bus to get you there.
3. Discounted drink prices. Crewbar beer and wine are super cheap—but don't over do it or they'll kick you off.
4. You will make friends from also many different countries and all continents!
5. You might visit amazing places (to name just a few) like Monte Carlo, Sydney, Venice, Florence, St. Petersburg, Tasmania, Nagasaki, New York, and a crew favorite, Cozumel, Mexico.
6. You will be an instrumental part of making someone else's vacation memorable. Guests will take pictures, want to stay in touch, and remember how you made their trip special.

7. You can go places others are not allowed. You can skip some lines here and there—you have your own gangway for getting on and off the ship, and access to secret (and quick) routes to different parts of the ship the guests never see.
8. There are learning resources available. Language lab will offer Rosetta Stone for languages, either to polish your English or learn another language. If you are interested in other positions onboard, there are often trainings you can attend to allow for advancement in other areas.
9. There are special crew activities onboard, ethically-oriented parties, and shore excursions to fun places in the ports. Sometimes there are sports events organized for competitions between crews of different ships in the same port (beach volleyball, table tennis, basketball, soccer, etc.)
10. Depending on your status, you may be allowed family or friends onboard as guests for free for a certain amount of time or be allowed hugely discounted rates. You may be allowed extra free time in this circumstance. This depends on your ship/company.

Got the idea? You've now gotten a glimpse of the ins and outs of life on a ship. So now it's up to you to assess the choice about whether this lifestyle suits you or not. What follows is advice from other working crew to further illuminate the lifestyle, effects, and potential advantages. No one can really explain how life onboard will affect everyone, and you too will have unique situations that will contribute to your particular life experience.

WORK AT SEA, SEE THE WORLD: AN INSIDER'S SECRETS TO THE WORKING LIFE ON A CRUISE SHIP

Welcome to your new life as a crew member! Enjoy the ride!

I leave you with this Apache blessing:
"May the sun bring you new energy by day.
May the moon softly restore you by night.
May the rain wash away your worries.
May the breeze blow new strength into your being.
May you walk gently through the world and
 know its beauty all the days of your life."

Bon Voyage!

CHAPTER 24

A Few Afterwords for the Over Forties

A note about being an over-forty crew member:
Any job onboard is typically aimed at the twenty-five to thirty-five-year-old candidates. As idyllic as it sometimes sounds, there are some emotional consequences to this life. Onboard you may have your close coworkers or bandmates to hang out with, but you are definitely in the minority. Others your age may be bridge officers or engineers, with whom you will rarely have contact unless you seek them out as they tend to circulate in their own worlds (unless you are one of them).

After-hours activities often involve hanging out in the crew bar as the hub for drinking and/or smoking. If these are not activities in which you find particular enjoyment, you may prefer to limit your participation to the crew events where there is dancing, ethnic food, or other entertainment provided, but just hanging out has its benefits in making new friends. Table tennis competitions and crew band jams can be a blast. But you may be wanting to head for bed before the action really gets started, which typically isn't until after 11:00 p.m.

Participation in guest activities is off limits, such as basketball, swimming, bumper cars, etc., unless there are special crew times reserved, so sticking to crew areas is it during off hours. The job has numerous demanding physical requirements. There is always *a lot* of walking from one end of the ship to another (some measure a good half-mile bow to stern), lots of steep stairs, and extra-heavy fire doors through which one must pass often. Some ships have no elevator to lower crew cabin decks, requiring one to lug heavy luggage down and up. If you're assigned to a room with bunk beds, this situation requires flexibility, strength, and balance to maneuver; you might need to convince yourself you're a ten-year-old again. Wherever you live onboard, it's a workout every day. If you have a solid support system at home, it will help emotionally, but you may find it isolating and sometimes a lonely endeavor. If you can build friendships (or relationships) onboard, you will find it more enjoyable, so regardless of the implied departmental segregations, mingle and get to know your fellow shipmates. Just remember, at this age, there is a new meaning to the term "pulling an all-nighter." No longer does it mean staying up all night to party, but now, it more often refers to that rare night that once you've gone to bed, you don't have to get up again to pee! And it's certainly more of a challenge on a bunk bed.

As a female, the challenges may be different than for men (see Mackenzie's notes above). There has been tremendous progress in terms of gender equality in this military hierarchy, but it is still a challenge for women to rise to the upper echelon of authority. There are several female ship captains, engineers, and bridge officers, but they have had to muster determination and fortitude to succeed. Among the general crew population, there is still a tendency by the men to view the new-hire females as "fresh meat," so beware. If you are an American, there may be a tendency for those of the opposite sex to be keen to make your acquaintance merely for your nationality connections in hopes of escaping their own countries' limitations, which may not offer them the life they seek. But many a happy relationship has blossomed among citizens of different countries that have had life-changing benefits—at any age!

But regardless of your position onboard, the challenges of ship life diminish as you stare out over the rail with the ship underway, watching a spectacular sunset, feeling the rush of the warm breeze on your face, feel the massive engines surging, and hear the rush of the waves on the hull. You marvel as you watch the wake churning the waves behind you, driving you toward yet another magical destination.

> **Life can be a shipwreck but we must not forget to sing in the lifeboats.**
>
> —Voltaire

ACKNOWLEDGMENTS

My sincerest appreciation for those who supported this effort, including the thousands of crew members who have added such joy to my life, and the many who specifically had a hand in being sure I had my facts straight.

David Morehead, my very first music director, still rocking the oceans with his magic trumpet.

Carlos Torres, the best cruise director on the ocean, a multitasker, and an amazingly talented human being.

My sister, Susan Anderson, who provided a warm and safe haven for my "home port."

My bandmates, Bruce Fernandes and Andrew Moss, who took a chance, helped me find my own voice and recharted the course of my life.

APPENDIX

General employment job site: *http://www.allcruisejobs.com*
Additional hiring-partner options: *https://cruisejobdirectory.com*
Contacts by corporation websites:

Carnival Corporation
(www.jobs.carnivalcorp.com)

> Carnival
> Princess
> Aida
> Costa
> Holland America
> P & O
> P & O Australia
> Cunard
> Seabourn

Royal Caribbean Cruise Lines
(www.Royal-Caribbean.ItsMyCareer.com; www.RoyalCaribbean.every-jobforme.com; www.jobs.RCLcareers.com; www.careers.royalcaribbean-group.com; www.cruiseshipjob.com; https://jobs.tuigroup.com)

> Royal Caribbean International
> Celebrity
> Azamara
> Pullmantur
> TUI

Norwegian Cruise Lines *(www.Norwegian-Cruise.ItsMyCareer.com; www.NCL.com/about/careers/shipboard-employment)*

    NCL
    Oceana
    Regent

Others:

MSC	*www.MSCCruiseShips.everyjobforme.com*
Disney	*www.Disney-Cruise-Line.ItsMyCareer.com*
	www.Jobs.DisneyCareers.com
Star Cruises (Asia)	*www.StarCruises.com*
Dream Cruises (Asia)	*www.Careers.dreamcruiseline.com*
Hurtigruten (Norway)	*www.Hurtigruten.com>about-hurtigruten>careers*
Viking	*www.employment.org>jobs>viking-cruises*
Virgin	*www.VirginVoyages.com>careers*
Silver Sea	*www.CrewCareer.silversea.com*
Celestyal (Greece)	*www.Celestyal.com*
Crystal Cruises	*www.CrystalCruises.com>careers*

Please note: availability of information on all sites is subject to change.

    Please support organizations that are dedicated to preserving the ocean, its wildlife, and protecting the earth's delicate climatic balance. Go to https://www.oceanconservancy.org. Please contribute for the benefit of us all. Thank you most sincerely!

MLC 2006 Regulation 2.3—Mandatory Hours of Work and Hours of Rest for Seafarers Requirements to Ensure that Seafarers have Regulated Hours of Work or Hours of Rest

MLC 2006 Regulation s://www.edumaritime.net/mic-2006/mic-regulation-2-32.3 deals with Hours of Work and Hours of Rest for Seafarers. Establishing either maximum hours of work or minimum hours of rest is essential in order to protect seafarers against fatigue due to excessive demands on their time and to ensure in the interests of safety, that hours of work and overtime (even if voluntary), in particular, does not exceed levels that are compatible with the safe and efficient discharge of duties on board.

The MLC 2006 provisions with respect to minimum hours of rest are, for the most part, reflected in the amendments to the IMO's STCW Convention that were adopted in June 2010. This means that it is likely that national provisions will already exist for seafarers covered by the STCW Convention.

The MLC 2006 requires that a country regulate either hours of work or hours of rest, in accordance with the parameters set out in Standard A 2.3. The Convention also provides information as to specific situations including drills, emergency situations and young seafarers.

The MLC 2006 defines "hours of work" as the time during which seafarers are requested to do work on account of the ship, while "hours of rest" means time outside hours of work which do not include short breaks. (*http://www.edumaritime.net/mic-2006/mic-regulatiom-2-3-work-rest-requirements*)

ABOUT THE AUTHOR

Nancy Soulé answers the numerous questions she had when she began her adventures as a cruise ship crew member in 2011. She has traveled to more than sixty countries, many of them repeatedly. With a background in theater, she is an author, jazz vocalist, voice-over artist, and public speaker. She also ship-hops as a theatrical wardrobe costumer, installing stage, aqua, and ice productions fleetwide. As a professional vocal coach, she especially enjoys helping speakers and singers to find their own unique voices, polish their presentation skills, and provide vocal recovery and stamina techniques. Look for information on her services as a voice-over artist and voice coach at http://soulesounds.webs.com and her other publications at http://www.nancysoule.net.

CPSIA information can be obtained
at www.ICGtesting.com
Printed in the USA
JSHW041136070423
39891JS00008B/22